Romantic Hawaiian Getaways

Romantic Hawaiian Getaways

LARRY FOX
BARBARA RADIN-FOX

John Wiley & Sons, Inc.
New York ❀ Chichester ❀ Brisbane ❀ Toronto ❀ Singapore

In recognition of the importance of preserving what has been written, it is a policy of John Wiley & Sons, Inc., to have books of enduring value published in the United States printed on acid-free paper, and we exert our best efforts to that end.

Published by John Wiley & Sons, Inc.

Library of Congress Cataloging in Publication Data

Fox, Larry, 1945–
    Romantic Hawaiian getaways / by Larry Fox and Barbara Radin-Fox.
      p.   cm.
    Includes index.
    ISBN 0-471-52538-3 (alk. paper)
    1. Hawaii—Description and travel—Guide-books.   I. Radin-Fox,
Barbara.   II. Title.
DU622.F69   1991
919.96904′4—dc20   91-287

Printed in the United States of America

10 9 8 7 6 5 4 3 2 1

For Peggy, Sandy, Dan, Steve, Marilyn, Bob, Julie, Marsha, and Jerry, who know who they are.

Acknowledgment

We gratefully thank Diana Reutter, who helped make this guide possible with her assistance, expertise, and guidance.

Contents

The crescent beach at Mauna Kea Beach Resort is the finest beach on Hawaii. *(Photo courtesy of Patti Cook & Associates)*

Introduction

*B*orn by fire, shaped by sea, wind, and rain, and enriched with some of the most unusual and beautiful plants imaginable, the beautiful islands of Hawaii are the closest we have to an Eden today.

On this Pacific paradise you can tour lush, green valleys filled with rainbows and veiled by mists created by towering waterfalls. You can see giant canyons—astonishingly deep ravines carved over the millennia by fast-rushing rivers coursing down from mysterious green mountains. You can stroll on beaches of white and black sand, stare in awe at rugged coastal mountains and ravines accessible only by air or sea, and gaze in wonder at some of the tallest mountains in the nation and the fiery volcanic forces that created them.

Hawaii was born 25 million years ago when volcanoes on the bottom of the Pacific Ocean began spewing forth immense quantities of lava. Over the millennia, these eruptions formed ever larger mountains that emerged from the sea.

As the centuries passed, these islands grew again through new eruptions, and began changing in another way. It began first on the wet, windward side of these barren lands. There, unusual plants and flowers, some now found only on these islands, found a fertile home in the lava fields. In time, these plants were joined by birds and small mammals, completing the island paradise. The only thing missing were people, but even that was to change.

Around the fifth century AD, a thousand years before Columbus's voyage, Polynesians sailed their double-hulled canoes from their South Pacific homes to these islands. Though their original home island is unknown, most experts believe it was what we now call Tahiti or the Marquesas.

It was an epic voyage, one made without the benefit of maps, navigational instruments, or any clear idea that there was even a place to go to. It is said they followed the flight of the Golden Plover, a bird known to the Polynesians as one that must bury its eggs on land.

The details of their 2,000-mile voyage are lost in time, but we know what they named the island paradise they discovered: Havaiki.

For more than a thousand years, no one else knew of their voyage, their discovery, or their new home. That all changed in the 1770s, an era when European sea captains explored the globe.

Captain James Cook and his ships *Resolution* and *Discovery* were crossing the Pacific on their way to North America when they came across the islands on January 18, 1778. "At this time we were in some doubt whether or not the land before us was inhabited," Cook wrote. "This doubt was soon cleared up . . ."

The islands were never the same. When Cook first saw them, the islands were separate kingdoms ruled by often-warring regents. Within 17 years after Cook's ships dropped anchor, the islands were united by King Kamehameha, who used European weapons and ships to conquer the islands of his opposing rulers.

After Cook (who was killed on a later voyage) came other Europeans: whalers, explorers, merchants, farmers, and missionaries.

Kamehameha and his descendants ruled for 98 years, until 1893 when Hawaii's last ruling monarch, Queen Liliuokalani, was removed from the throne by American businessmen who opposed her strong rule and independent ways. In January 1893, American business leaders, assisted by U.S. troops stationed at the U.S. base in Pearl Harbor, declared a new provisional government replacing that of the queen. President Grover Cleveland called the takeover "a great wrong," and sought congressional action to restore the queen to power. Congress, caught up in the fever of *Manifest Destiny*, ignored Cleveland.

On July 4, 1894 Sanford Dole, a descendant of missionaries, became president of the new Republic of Hawaii. Followers of the queen tried one last time to overthrow Dole's government,

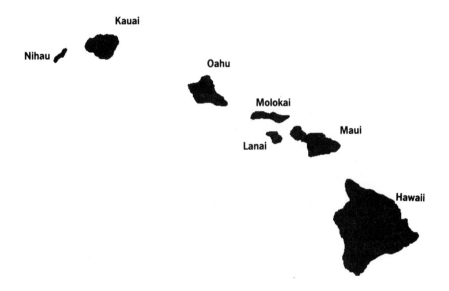

Kauai

Nihau

Oahu

Molokai

Lanai

Maui

Hawaii

The Islands of Hawaii

and when that failed the queen was imprisoned for more than a year.

The new republic was short lived. In July 1898, the Congress annexed the islands, and in 1900 the islands became an official U.S. territory. From then to December 7, 1941, Hawaii was an agricultural center, known for its sugar cane and a new crop called pineapples planted on Lanai by James D. Dole, a cousin of Sanford Dole.

It was the huge naval base at Pearl Harbor that changed American perceptions of the distant islands. The Japanese attack on the base seared the name of Pearl Harbor, Hawaii, and Honolulu forever in the American psyche. The attack also eventually disproved one argument used against granting statehood to the islands, that the population—predominantly Japanese, Filipinos, and other Asians—could never be loyal American citizens. The 442d Regimental Combat Team, composed of more than 3,000 volunteers of Japanese heritage, fought bravely and fiercely in Italy and France, winning seven presidential unit citations and thousands of individual medals.

By the 1950s, the question of statehood for the territory of Hawaii was not whether, but when. Finally, on March 12, 1959, the islands of Hawaii were finally welcomed as a full member of the union.

In the decades since, despite all the changes that jet airplanes, statehood, and the tourist boom have wrought on these islands, Hawaii remains a beautiful land of sharp contrasts. Hawaii, the Big Island, may have the world's most active volcanoes, but it also has snow-capped peaks that reach more than two miles high. Oahu has the greatest population and attracts even more millions of visitors to its famed Waikiki Beach resort strip, but it also has isolated regions laced with quaint and colorful towns and softened by lush gardens and forests. Tiny Lanai may be a branch office of a modern American conglomerate, but it is almost deserted (only 2,300 residents) and barely developed (millions of pineapples, but only three hotels).

Maui is busy and sophisticated, but it has valleys filled with waterfalls and exotic plants, and mountain regions that resemble a scene from the moon. Molokai is large yet bucolic, its lovely green fields isolated atop the tallest coastal bluffs in the islands. And Kauai, the Garden Isle, not only has a mountain that gets more rain than any other place on earth, but it also has a dry side where cactus bloom.

Amid all this magnificence are special places—fine resorts and charming inns, intimate restaurants serving excellent and creative dishes—and opportunities for the experience of a lifetime.

As we have done in our other guidebooks, we emphasize throughout this book the Hawaiian locales we found most romantic. The hotels, resorts, and inns we choose are all, in one way or another, special; they have qualities that we found attractive, creative, and interesting. The restaurants were selected because of their high quality of food as well as their ambience.

In addition, for each island we describe a tour of the places of beauty and adventure. Chapter 7 describes adventures that are exciting and unusual: dinner in a king's palace, picnics at an isolated grove next to a waterfall deep within a rain forest, small boat tours of some of the most dramatic and beautiful coastline in the world, sunset cruises, snorkeling and diving expeditions, and journeys into the mouth of a volcano.

All these things—the uncommon beauty of the land, the romantic and luxurious hotels and resorts, and the delightful opportunities for fun and adventure—make the island paradise of Hawaii a place for romance, a place where dreams can come true.

The Hawaiians have a word for it, a word that means welcome as well as farewell. It also means love.

Aloha.

CHAPTER 1

Hawaii: The Big Island

*F*rom the air, the landscape of Hawaii is extraordinary: giant rivers of black swirl and flow their way down from the mountains, crossing the coastal plains before meeting the sea. The rivers of black are ancient lava flows from the most unusual island in the Hawaiian chain. The lava fields are only part of the striking scenery to be found on the youngest—and still growing— of the islands.

Hawaii can only be described with superlatives. The Big Island, as it is known, is the youngest of the islands in the Hawaiian chain, and is still being formed as its seemingly inexhaustible inner volcanic forces spew forth ever more lava. It is the largest island; with 4,038 square miles, it is twice as big as the rest of its sister islands put together. It has two of the nation's tallest peaks: Mauna Kea (13,796 feet above sea level) and Mauna Loa (13,667 feet above sea level); Mauna Loa is one of two active volcanoes on the island. It has the most variety in landscapes: rain forests, grasslands studded with cactus, tropical beaches, snow-capped mountains, coastal plains covered with lava flows— some centuries old and others still simmering with heat—mist-shrouded valleys, broad fields filled with crops—such as coffee, macadamia nuts and bananas—and awesome windswept canyons dividing mountains almost a mile high.

More importantly, Hawaii is filled with beautiful and romantic places: the gardens of Hilo and the many nurseries where orchids and exotic plants are grown, the rugged jungle mountains and valleys of the north coast, the black sand beaches, and the fabulous resorts.

And there is more, those sights that are so unusual that they cannot be missed: the volcanoes and the enormous fields of ancient lava flows; the heiaus—ancient temples of refuge—where wrongdoers could be purified and escape the wrath of Hawaii's kings; the observatories where romance-seeking couples can get even closer to the stars; the cactus-studded rangelands of the Parker Ranch, one of the largest private ranches in the world; and the many quaint and colorful towns around the island.

The Big Island is too large to tour in a few days. To fully explore its wonders would take at least a week. The following description breaks Hawaii down into manageable districts and should help you decide where to begin.

Hilo and the Northeast Coast

Any tour of the eastern coast should begin at Hilo, the largest city on the island. Hilo is on the rainy coast of the island—140 inches fall here each year—and the main attractions for visitors are its lush gardens and parks near its waterfront and the orchid and exotic plant nurseries in and around town. Although much of the precipitation falls at night, you may need to carry an umbrella during a daytime tour.

Hilo has about 42,000 residents, but remains a slow-paced town that hasn't really outgrown its role as the commercial center of the sugarcane plantations surrounding it. Although Hilo is small, a map will help you tour the town and the surrounding countryside. Stop by the Hawaii Visitors' Bureau at 180 Kinoole Street for a map and other information.

The main park in town is along the waterfront, which was destroyed in 1946, rebuilt, and then destroyed again in 1960 by *tsunamis* (tidal waves). Banyan Drive, a road that curves around the Waiakea peninsula, is the location of many of Hilo's hotels. The drive gets its name from the banyan trees that were planted along it by numerous celebrities in the 1930s (the plaques on the trees identify them), and is a pleasant place for a walk or drive. A bridge on the peninsula leads to Coconut Island, a quiet park that once was a sanctuary used for healing and birthing ceremonies.

On the Waiakea peninsula are the Liliuokalani Gardens, 30 acres of landscaped gardens, Japanese pagodas, bridges, and a teahouse. The garden is beautiful but its origin is tinged with

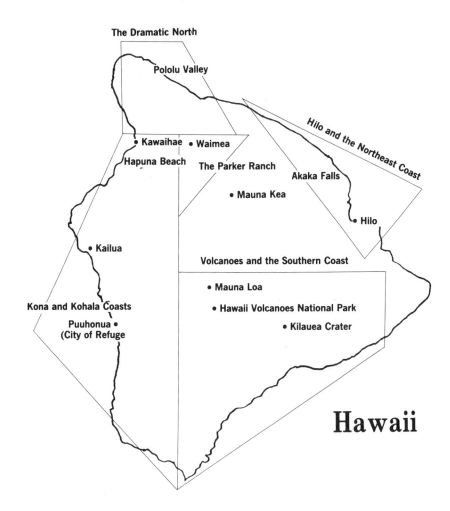

The Dramatic North

Pololu Valley

Hilo and the Northeast Coast

• Kawaihae   • Waimea

Hapuna Beach   The Parker Ranch

Akaka Falls

• Mauna Kea

• Hilo

• Kailua

Volcanoes and the Southern Coast

• Mauna Loa

Kona and Kohala Coasts

• Hawaii Volcanoes National Park

Puuhonua •
(City of Refuge

• Kilauea Crater

Hawaii

sadness. The terrible tidal wave of May 22, 1960 destroyed the buildings in this area. After the devastation, the land was turned into a park to serve as a safety zone.

The Banyan Drive leads to Lihiwai Street and the Suisan Fish Market, a colorful and busy bazaar where seafood of all types is sold on weekday mornings at a frantic auction conducted in several languages. After the market, turn right on Kamehameha Avenue and cross the Wailoa River—the shortest river in the world at one-half a mile in length. The river leads to a park and larger pond, a visitors' center, and some beautifully landscaped grounds.

Except for the parks, downtown Hilo is rather unexceptional. Perhaps the most interesting building is the Lyman Missionary House and Museum at 276 Haili Street. The house was built in 1839 by the Reverend David Belden Lyman, and is furnished with pieces and curios from that era. The adjacent museum has exhibits on the various immigrant groups that populate the island, artifacts, and lava and minerals. The museum also offers unusual one-hour narrated tours of Hilo in an open-sided 1948 Plymouth ($5 per person).

A block away, in front of the library at 300 Waianuenue Avenue, are the Naha and Pinao stones, two large stones that hold their own tales. The Pinao stone is said to have been the pillar for an ancient temple on the site, while the Naha stone plays a far more important role. Legend has it that whoever could move the 5,000-pound stone would become king of all the islands. King Kamehameha, who indeed united the islands under his rule, moved the stone while still a teenager, according to island lore.

Some of Hawaii's beauty may be found in one of the craft, art, and antiques galleries of Keawe Street, a block away inland from the intersection of Kamehameha and Waianuenue avenues. Indonesian textiles, masks, paintings, and other crafts can be found at the Gamelan Gallery at 227 Keawe Street. The Cunningham Gallery at 116 Keawe Street offers some fine Hawaiian artwork, and the Most Irresistible Shop in Hilo at 110 Keawe Street sells fine lace napkins, dolls, toys, jewelry, and other items.

More art can be found at the East Hawaii Cultural Center, at 141 Kalakaua Street. The building, a curious mixture of art deco and traditional Hawaiian building styles, houses art galleries and artists' studios, and holds workshops.

The nearby Potter's Gallery at 95 Waianuenue Avenue has some nice baskets, jewelry, and raku earthenware made by Hilo artisans. And at Hawaiian Handcraft, at 760 Kilauea Avenue, you can buy bowls and boxes made from koa and other rare and beautiful wood.

The true natural beauty of the Big Island's east coast is found outside of Hilo. Three miles east of town, on Highway 12 (Kalanianaole Avenue) is Onekahakaha Beach Park, where you will find a one-mile-long white sand beach and picnic facilities. The James Keohola Beach Park, a mile farther, and Leleiwi Beach Park, another mile east on Highway 12, have fine beaches for swimming and sunbathing.

Wailuka River State Park, off Waianuenue Avenue just west of town, has two magnificent waterfalls. Rainbow Falls creates a beautiful rainbow that is best viewed in the morning when the morning sun first strikes the mist. A trail from the lookout leads to a private picnic area. (Note: Waianuenue Avenue is one-way into Hilo from 7:15 AM–8:00 AM weekdays.)

The other falls are called Boiling Pots, despite the presence of a sign saying they are the Peepee Falls. By whatever name, the falls are a series of lava bowls, linked by the churning waters. The pots look like giant jacuzzis, bubbling into pools of foamy liquid, but be wary about getting in. The currents can be dangerous.

Perhaps the most romantic flower (save the rose) is the delicate and exotic orchid. There are more than 20,000 varieties of orchids on Hawaii, and most of them grow around Hilo because of the large amounts of rain on the east coast. These colorful plants can be seen at the Hilo Orchidarium, 524 Manono Street, and Hilo Tropical Gardens, 1477 Kalanianaole Avenue, which has two acres of orchid gardens, tidal pools, and other unusual and beautiful flowers and plants. Kualoa Farms, at Mamaki and

Kealakai streets, has 62 acres of gardens, featuring orchids and more than 20 acres of anthuriums. Guided tours are scheduled daily. The Nani Mau Gardens, off Highway 11 at 421 Makalika Street, has more than 2,000 varieties of orchids and more than 100 different tropical fruit trees and bushes.

Farther out of town, the Akatsuka Orchid Gardens, on Highway 11 at the 22-mile marker between Hilo and Volcano, displays and sells orchids in its beautiful gardens. All these nurseries and gardens are open daily; some require a small admission.

Three main roads lead out from Hilo to the rest of the island. Highway 19 heads northeast along the Hamakua Coast. Seven miles out of Hilo is the turnoff for the coastal road, a four-mile drive filled with beautiful scenery and stunning views of the sea. The old yellow church you pass is the office of the Hawaii Tropical Botanical Garden, a 17-acre garden with more than 1,000 species of exotic plants and flowers, waterfalls, and lily ponds filled with Japanese koi, or carp. The road leads back to Highway 19, where you continue north to the left-hand turnoff at Honomu for Akaka Falls State Park, a 66-acre garden featuring ginger, orchids, azaleas and other plants. There is a trail leading through the forest to the 420-foot-high Akaka Falls and the smaller (100 feet), but no less beautiful, Kapuna Falls. About 50 miles out of Hilo is Honokaa, the macadamia nut capital of the world, and just beyond that is Kukuihaele, a seafront village famous for its local crafts. Waipio Woodworks sells interesting wooden artworks, paintings, and other creations.

Highway 200 (the Saddle Road) is a slow, often difficult road that cuts across the island near Mauna Kea before turning north to the Kohala region. Mauna Kea is worth a visit, for it is said to be the finest location in the world for stargazing. Follow Highway 200 for 30 miles west of Hilo until you come to an access road leading to the Onizuka Center for International Astronomy and the summit at 13,796 feet. The summit holds numerous observatories, and free tours are offered at 2:00 PM and 6:30 PM Saturday and at 2:00 PM Sunday. Reservations may be required; call 808/935–3371. Two cautions: first, the climate at sea level may be tropical, but on the summit it is freezing, so dress appropriately. Second, you will need a four-wheel drive vehicle to reach the summit.

Another attraction atop Mauna Kea is skiing during the winter months. The skiing is for very experienced skiers only, and there are no lifts or other ski facilities. Diehards can call Ski Guides Hawaii (808/885–4188) to arrange a lift via snowmobile to the snow-covered peak.

The main road to the west coast and the southern region of the island is Highway 11. When you leave Hilo on Highway 11 take time to turn right on the Stainback Highway for the short drive to the Panaewa Rain Forest Zoo, which features animals and plants only found in rain forests. Then return back to Highway 11 and turn south to the Puna District, a region known for the golden papayas grown there and one of nature's most awesome attractions—active volcanoes.

Volcanoes and the Southern Coast

Volcanoes created the Hawaiian Islands, and their presence is nowhere more noticeable than on the southern coast of the Big Island. This is the Puna District, an incredible world of solid seas of black, broken by vents seething sulfurous fumes and occasional fields of fire.

When you reach Highway 130, turn off on it and drive about nine miles to the marked overlook. From here you can walk into the field of black volcanic cones and rifts that was a site of a massive lava flow in 1955. You can walk on the huge sea of lava, but caution should be taken.

For an even more bizarre sight, turn left on Highway 132 at Pahoa and drive to Lava Tree State Park. Here you can see molds of trees created when a 1790 lava flow covered a forest. The molds—some as tall as an adult—look like black smokestacks, and were formed when molten lava surrounded a tree trunk and then cooled, creating the "chimney." It's an eerie sight.

HAWAIIAN LANGUAGE PRIMER

Words in Hawaii look strange to the eye and sound even stranger to the ears of nonislanders. That's because the Hawaiian alphabet contains only 12 letters: the 5 vowels and 7 consonants (h, k, l, m, n, p, and w). The trick to pronouncing Hawaiian words is to pronounce every letter separately. Vowel sounds are: *a* as in *army*, *e* as in *every*, *i* as the ee in *see*, *o* as in *gold*, *u* as the *oo* in *mood*. In dipthongs (*ei, eu, oi, ai, ae, ao,* and *au*), stress the first member (i.e., lei).

Consonants are pronounced the same as in English except for *w*, which is pronounced as *w* when it is the first letter of a word but as a *v* when it follows the vowels *e* or *i*.

If you see an apostrophe in a word, it means that the letter *k* has been omitted and you pronounce it with a break in sound between the letters it separates.

Here are some possibly familiar and some not so familiar Hawaiian words that you will undoubtedly hear and see while visiting the islands:

Return back to Highway 130 and turn left again toward the coast. Kaimu Black Sand Beach, on Highway 137 just east of the intersection with Highway 130, is stunning, a picture-perfect curved beach fringed with palms. The scenery is beautiful and seems too perfect to be true; swimming there is dangerous because of the currents. Two miles farther is the Star of the Sea Painted Church, a small white-steepled chapel whose interior is decorated in colorful frescoes.

(Note: Recent lava flows have cut off Highway 130 between Kaimu Beach and Hawaii Volcanoes National Park. Check with local authorities on the status of the highway.)

Return north on Highway 130 to Highway 11, turn left and continue on to Hawaii Volcanoes National Park. The park, about 30 miles southwest of Hilo, covers 344 square miles and has two

aloha—greetings,
   welcome, farewell, love
aloha nui loa—much love
hale—house
ha'ina—end of song
hana—work
haole—caucasian
heiau—temple
hele mai—come here
hauoli la Hanau—happy
   birthday
ho'olaule'a—celebration
huhu—angry
ipo—sweetheart, lover
kahuna—priest, expert
kama'aina—native born
kane—man, used on
   men's room doors

kapu—forbidden, keep out
lanai—porch, veranda
lei—garland, wreath
mahalo—thanks
makai—toward the sea
malihini—stranger,
   newcomer
mauna—mountain
mele—song
moana—ocean
mu'umu'u—loose-fitting
   dress
paniolo—cowboy
pehea'oe—how are you?
waihini—woman, the word
   on the women's room
   door
wikiwiki—fast, hurry

active volcanoes—Mauna Loa and Kilauea—and the accompanying landscape, rain forests, and rare plants and animals.

The park is open 24 hours a day. Between 8:30 AM and 4:30 PM daily, there is an admission fee ($5 per car, $2 for pedestrians and bicyclists, free for seniors). At other times admission is free for everyone.

Just inside the park entrance is the Kilauea Visitors' Center, with movies and exhibits on the volcanoes. Next door is the Volcano Art Center, built in 1877 as a lodge. The center features the work of photographers and artists who took the volcanoes as their subjects, and a small array of arts and crafts.

Volcano House, across from the center, is a lodge and restaurant. You can stay there in one of the 38 rooms or dine in the Ka Ohelo restaurant. The snack bar at Volcano House overlooks the Kilauea Caldera and its fiery center, the Halemaumau Crater. There is no danger; the last eruption from this crater was in 1924, and the most recent eruptions from Kilauea are from vents and cones lower on its slopes.

On the crater rim you may make an offering to Madame Pele, the volcano goddess. This deity attracts offerings of all kinds, from beer cans to flowers.

From these buildings you can walk or drive the 1.1 miles around the entire crater. The scenery is spectacular. The crater is huge—2.5 miles long, 2 miles wide, and 400 feet deep. The air is filled with sulfur fumes, which smell like rotten eggs and may be hazardous to those with respiratory difficulties. About halfway around the crater is the Thomas A. Jaggar Museum, with some fascinating films of recent eruptions and seismographs that indicate the underground turbulence is unabated.

Three trails lead from the museum: Devastation Trail, a 30-minute stroll on a boardwalk over eerie landscape including a skeleton forest created by a 1959 eruption; Halemaumau Overlook, a 10-minute walk to another view of the crater; and Thurston Lava Tube, a 20-minute walk through a fern glade and a natural tunnel created by the lava.

Back at the lodges, the Chain of Craters Road covers 24 miles (and descends almost 4,000 feet) and it circles all the old volcanic craters. The trip takes several hours to complete, because of the turns and the often stunning views, for which you will want to stop and gaze in awe.

The best way to view the park and any eruption and lava flow in progress is from the air, by helicopter. Volcano Heli-Tours (808/967–7578) flies out of Volcano, the small town on Highway 11 just east of the park. The fee is usually about $100 per person. Other helicopter and airplane tour companies operate out of Hilo and from the other island airports. (See Chapter 7 for details.)

Highway 11 leads southwest from the park to the Kau District, a far more hospitable landscape where macadamia nuts, sugarcane, and other crops grow on prosperous plantations. The highway passes through several small towns that are picturesque but offer little for tourists. The black sand beach at Punaluu Beach Park, about eight miles beyond Pahala is beautiful. Twenty miles farther on Highway 15 is the turnoff on the South Point Road, which will take you through some rugged countryside to a wind-swept cape that is the southernmost point in the United States.

The Kona and Kohala Coasts

The west coast of Hawaii is where the best beaches, the biggest resorts, and the hordes of tourists can be found. It is also a region of a more subtle beauty than Hilo's gardens or Puna's black seas of lava. On the west coast, wiry grasses battle for supremacy with the barren fields of lava, white sand beaches beckon to swimmers, and ancient temples tell tales about life in Hawaii before the first Europeans came.

Highway 11 runs up and down the coast, and this tour should start at the southern end, where the previous section left off.

South of Kealia, Highway 11 enters two marvels of nature: giant lava flows from Mauna Loa and the Honaunau Forest, and a 100,000-acre park of tropical ash and Australian red ginger trees. Continue north on Highway 11 and turn left at Keokea on Highway 160 and drive about three miles to St. Benedict's Church, one of the more beautiful churches in the islands. The interior of this small, 90-year-old church is covered with frescoes and murals. The artwork was the creation of Father John Berchmans Velghe, a Belgian who wanted his flock to enjoy the beauty of a European cathedral.

The road from St. Benedict's heads down to the sea and Puuhonua O Honaunau, a sacred place that was a refuge for lawbreakers and those who feared the wrath of Hawaii's kings. Until King Kamehameha II's rule in the early nineteenth century, this place and others like it in the island served as havens for lawbreakers, who were allowed to live within the city walls under the protection of priests. After a purification ritual, the wrongdoers were allowed to leave the refuge, protected by the amnesty granted by the priests.

The temple was razed in 1829, when the Hawaiians changed their old ways. Today the site is a 180-acre national park. The wall surrounding the refuge and the temple called Hale-O-Keawe Heiau were rebuilt. Demonstrations of ancient Hawaiian skills, games, and entertainment are often held in the park.

The seafront road leading north from Puuhonua O Honaunau crosses the Keei plain, a barren area of lava and grass that was the battlefield in 1780 when Kamehameha's forces defeated those of local ruler Kiwalo. Beyond the battlefield is Napoopoo, a small fishing village on Kealakekua Bay, where Captain James Cook, the European discoverer of the islands, was killed in 1799 while trying to halt a battle between his men and the natives.

The road leads out of Napoopoo, back upland to Highway 11, passing through coffee plantations where the strong Kona beans are grown. If you turn south on Highway 11, you will soon come to Honaunau and the Kona Country Fair, where everything from eelskin wallets and flowers to shell jewelry and T-shirts is sold. It is open Wednesdays, Fridays, and Saturdays from 8:00 AM to 4:00 PM.

Take Highway 11 north again to Highway 180, where you turn off for a ten-mile drive to Holualoa, where the Kona Arts Center is located in the old Holualoa Congregational Church and, across the road, the Coffee Mill Workshop. Both galleries display paintings, batik, and other creations, and the artists are often there working on new pieces.

From Highway 180 several roads lead down the coast to Kailua-Kona, a town with a regal history and many names. Its real name is Kailua, but there are towns called Kailua on Oahu and Maui. The U.S. Postal Service calls it Kailua-Kona, but residents call it Kona. Adding to the confusion is the airport north of town, formally called Ke'ahole Airport but known more familiarly to residents and ticket agents as Kona.

The town's history is linked to King Kamehameha, who

spent his final years there. The king's palace grounds are on the tiny peninsula next to the Hotel King Kamehameha, located at 75-5660 Palani Road next to the fishing wharf in the center of town. The palace was the center of Kamehameha's rule from 1813 to 1819, when he died. The compound has been restored and includes Ahuena Heiau, a lava platform that holds thatched huts and wooden statues of gods. The hotel conducts free tours at 3:00 PM Friday and 1:30 PM the rest of the week.

Farther around the waterfront, at 75-5718 Alii Drive, is another royal building, the Hulihee Palace. This two-story building was constructed in 1838 by island Governor John Adams Kuakini and used by King David Kalakaua as a summer palace in the late 1800s. The palace is now a museum with artifacts on royal lifestyles.

The waterfront is where you can sign up for deep-sea fishing trips, romantic sunset cruises, or voyages on the *Atlantis IV*, a 65-foot-long submarine designed like a sightseeing bus that takes you down to a coral reef. You can sign up for the submarine ride at the Hotel King Kamehameha or by calling 808/329–6626. Tour prices are about $60 for adults, $32 for children.

Another seasonal attraction is the whaling cruise that begins at the wharf. Between December and April, Pacific Whale Foundations (808/329–3522 or 800/WHALE-1-1) runs charter boats to see the annual migration of humpback whales. It's an awesome sight; one that should not be missed.

Alii Drive and the other streets in this section of Kailua-Kona are busy with traffic and pedestrians. Many of the small hotels are located here, along with numerous shops and restaurants. While many sell tourist items—T-shirts, bags, souvenirs, and shell leis—some offer beautiful arts and crafts made on the island. Alapaki's Hawaiian Things, in the Keahou Shopping Village at 76-6831 Alii Drive, sells some fine crafts, including the rare (and expensive) leis made of Nihau shells.

After strolling down the streets and waterfront, take Highway 19 north out of town. The road again crosses enormous fields of lava. Many of the lava flows here date back to the eruption of

Mt. Hualalai around 1800. One oddity you will notice on this landscape of black is the Big Island's form of graffiti. On the black lava boulders and walls on the side of the highway you will see graffiti—happy faces, artistic designs, John Loves Susan, for example—made up of hundreds of small white pebbles. It's striking, and some displays are quite creative and witty.

The highway then takes you past some of the finest resorts on the island. The famous Hyatt Regency Waikoloa, the thatched huts of Kona Village, and the super luxury resorts—Mauna Lani, Ritz-Carlton, Mauna Kea—and their lavish boutiques are located here. The beaches range from superb to nonexistent. Although by law all beaches in Hawaii are open to the public, the resorts can make it difficult, by either charging stiff parking fees or barring your car from entering the grounds and making you walk to the beach over the lava fields. A simpler option is to visit Hapuna State Recreation Area (watch for the sign between the Mauna Kea Beach and Mauna Lani hotels), which has one of the better beaches on the island.

Just north of Mauna Kea Beach, take Highway 270 when it branches off toward Kawaihae and follow signs to the Puukohola Visitor Center. Two ancient Hawaiian temples (heiaus) built during the rule of King Kamehameha are on this site. The Puukohola Heiau, a massive (224 feet by 100 feet) fortresslike platform originally built around 1550 and reconstructed by Kamehameha in 1790–91, was dedicated to the war god. Playing the main role in the sacrifice was the king's main rival on the island, Keoua Kuahuula, although it's doubtful that he was a willing player. A short walk away is the smaller Mailekini Heiau and Spencer Beach Park, which has a nice white sand beach and gentle waters for swimmers.

The Dramatic North

The road north, Highway 270, is a drive that says much about the geography and climate of Hawaii. As you drive north from Kawaihae, you leave a rugged landscape of black lava and brown

LIGHT RAYS AND MANTA RAYS

A nightly show at the Mauna Kea Beach resort takes place at Manta Ray Point, a stone-walled lookout downhill from the main hotel. At night, bright lights are turned on, sending a field of light on the sea below. The light attracts plankton, which in turn attracts manta rays. Mantas are large, black-and-white rays that move with the grace of a ballerina despite being almost the size of a compact car.

The giant rays sail gracefully through the lighted water, moving through the sea by flapping their wings like a lazy bird. Their circling dance—that's the most fitting word, for it is so graceful—while they feed on the plankton is an unparalleled show of a natural wonder. It is unforgettable.

grasses and enter a green world filled with lush vegetation and almost unspoiled by development.

About 12 miles north of Kawaihae is Lapahaki State Historic Park, where archeologists have partially restored a 600-year-old fishing village. The small houses, gardens, cemetery, and shrines are enchanting, for they give a glimpse into how the average Hawaiian lived centuries ago.

A bit farther north is Mahukona, a nearly abandoned shipping port with a fine beach, and farther on is Kapaa Beach Park, a great place for snorkeling even though there is no sand beach.

Another of Hawaii's heiaus (temples) can be found by taking the turnoff for Upolo Airfield down to the coast. Mookini Heiau, built around AD 480, was a sacrificial temple, and part of the walls and temple platform can still be seen.

From this point Highway 270 turns east and passes through three colorful towns and an overlook that offers a view of some of the most dramatic scenery on the island.

The first village is Hawi, a former plantation town with some quaint houses and churches. Just beyond is Kapaau, where a gilt-and-bronze statue of King Kamehameha stands in front of the courthouse. The statue was lost at sea but was somehow found again and placed in Kapaau, which is near Kamehameha's birthplace.

The best attraction in town is the Kalahikiola Church, created by the missionaries in the region who also started the sugar plantations. The church was built in 1855 by Hawaiians using local materials. Also on the grounds, beyond the archway, are the small frame schoolhouses that once housed the Kohala Girls' School.

East of town is Niulii, a small community almost swallowed by the jungle, and 1.5 miles farther at the end of Highway 270 is the Pololu Valley Overlook, one of the more spectacular vistas on the island. From here you can take a 45-minute walk down a trail to an isolated black sand beach.

After the overlook return on Highway 270 to Hawi, turn south on Highway 250 and drive 20 miles south to Waimea and one of the world's largest private ranches.

The Parker Ranch

Waimea is a town that sits between two distinctly different island regions. On all sides but the south, the land is green and mountainous. To the south is the plateau that reaches to Mauna Kea, an area of black lava flows, scrub trees, tan range grasses, and occasional cactus.

This striking difference is caused by the winds, which sweep over the Kohala Mountains to the north, causing the moisture-laden clouds to dump their rain on the hills and Waimea.

It was in these green hills that John Palmer Parker established his ranch, which now encompasses some 250,000 acres. In 1809, Parker was a 19-year-old sailor who quit the sea to round up stray cattle for King Kamehameha I. In time, Parker acquired his own herd and, more importantly, married the king's granddaughter. Today the Parker Ranch has an estimated 50,000 head of cattle worked by *paniolos* (cowboys) on horseback.

Waimea is a ranch town located at the foot of the Kohala Mountains. In recent years it has been discovered by well-to-do outsiders, many of whom bought miniranches and homes in the hills outside of town. These new residents have attracted developers to build new shopping centers, fancy restaurants, galleries, and boutiques.

Tours of the Parker Ranch start from the Parker Ranch Visitor Center and Museum, at the Parker Ranch Shopping Center at highways 19 and 190 in the heart of Waimea. There you can see a video on the ranch and book a three-hour tour, with lunch, to see the ranch and the paniolos. (Shorter tours are available 9:00 AM to 4:00 PM daily except Sunday, and the cost varies from $15–$38 for adults, $8–$20 for children. Call 808/885–7655.)

On the tour you will see Mana, the koa-wood house of the John Palmer Parker family, and Puuopelu, the nineteenth-century home of the Smart family, where current Parker Ranch owner Richard Smart has his large collection of art and antiques. Though Smart is the owner, he prefers acting in cabarets and musicals on Oahu to managing the enormous ranch.

The Parker presence spreads beyond town. Where highways 19 and 250 meet is the Kamuela Museum, where Parker descendants Albert and Harriet Solomon display their collection of Hawaiiana and other artifacts.

Waimea is an attraction, even for those without any interest in ranches. The Hale Kea Shopping Center on Highway 19, a creation of millionaire Laurance Rockefeller and located on his former ranch, holds some interesting shops, while Parker Square, a small U-shaped complex of frame buildings painted red and trimmed with white, holds gourmet food shops and antique and craft galleries. Try the Gallery of Great Things, which has some stunning items made of koa wood, or the Waimea General Store, an old-fashioned trove of pottery, soaps, scents, candies, and other gift items.

Another fine shop is Yugen, in Spencer House on Highway

19, where batik artist Carolyn Ainsworth sells her stylish silk dresses, linen jackets, and accessories.

These shops are very nice, but in a region known for cattle, cactus, rodeos, and cowboys, they seem so out of place.

For More Information

The airports, hotels, and rental car companies have a wide variety of maps, driving guides, brochures, current-event magazines, and other publications. Pick them up and use them.

The Hawaii Visitors' Bureau also has booths at most major airports. For more information, contact them at 180 Kinoole St., Suite 104, Hilo, HI 96720 (808/961–5767) and at 75–5719 W. Alii Dr., Kailua-Kona, HI 96740 (808/329–7787).

Festivals

Cherry Blossom Festival—A celebration of Japanese culture and heritage, featuring music, dance, and food. Late February/early March.

Merrie Monarch Festival—A week-long hula competition. It begins the Saturday after Easter.

Buddha Day—A pageant of flowers with parades and other activities. April.

Lei Day—Celebration of the flower lei with music, hula, food, and sales of fantastic leis. May 1.

King Kamehameha Day—Parades, fairs, and other activities honor the king who united the islands. June.

International Festival of the Pacific—Music, dance, and food from Asia and Polynesia. July.

Parker Ranch Rodeo—Paniolos from the Parker Ranch and other Big Island ranches compete in this major rodeo. July.

Bon Odori Season—Buddhist festival that honors ancestors with music and dance. Late July/August.

Aloha Week—A celebration of Hawaii's culture, with music, dance, parades, crafts, food, and more. September/October.

King Kalakaua Kupuna and Keiki Hula Festival—Hula contests for all ages. November.

For more information about the festivals and the exact dates, contact the visitors' information offices listed above.

Where to Stay

Choosing the right hotel and resort is not merely a matter of money. What's romantic and interesting for you may not be so for someone else. Some resorts are big and busy—perhaps too much so for some. And some hotels and inns may be too quiet and too inconvenient, if all you want to do is sit on the beach. The resorts, hotels, and inns listed here are special places. Our price breakdown is as follows:

Expensive—$200 or more a night for a standard double room
Moderate—$100 to $199 a night for a standard double room
Inexpensive—Less than $100 a night for a standard double room.

At some resorts, meal plans are available that may save you money. The drawback is that the MAP (Modified American Plan) restricts your flexibility in trying restaurants elsewhere.

Hilo and the East Coast

Even though this area is filled with natural beauty, Hilo itself doesn't have a lot of romantic and beautiful inns and hotels. Try these:

Hamakua Hideaway—This one-bungalow B & B is perfect for those seeking privacy. It has a kitchen, one bedroom, and a fantastic view of the spectacular Hamakua coast as well as a lovely waterfall just below the cabin. The drawback is the mosquitoes. Inexpensive. P.O. Box 5104, Kukuihaele, HI 96727. 808/775-7425.

Hawaii Naniloa Hotel—Just renovated, this is Hilo's finest hotel. The large complex—386 rooms in two towers—is surrounded by gardens on the shore of Hilo Bay. The rooms offer views of either Mauna Kea or the ocean and are comfortable and nicely furnished, but not exceptional. Facilities include two pools, including one in the health spa, four tennis courts, and an adjacent golf course. Inexpensive/moderate. 93 Banyan Dr., Hilo, HI 96720. 808/969–3333 or 800/367–5360.

Hilo Hawaiian Hotel—The views of Mauna Kea, Coconut Island, Hilo Bay, and the surrounding countryside are spectacular at this 290-room resort. The beauty, though, is more outside than inside, for the color scheme is a bit strange—red, white, and blue. The rooms are comfortable and nicely furnished in island style with rattan. Facilities include a pool. Inexpensive. 71 Banyan Dr., Hilo, HI 96720. 808/935–9361 or 800/367–5004.

Around the Volcanoes:

The House at Kapoho—If you like remoteness and privacy, something like a rustic cottage on the edge of a lagoon in a grove of tropical trees, this two-bedroom house may be the romantic getaway for you. The house is in Kapoho, on the eastern tip of the island. The grounds are gorgeous: coconut and hala trees surround the lagoon (which is shared with two rarely home neighbors), a pool is just steps downhill and a rock beach is a few minutes walk away. The house is airy and comfortable. Bring your own drinking water (there is a well for other water), and don't expect a TV or phone. Inexpensive. Write care of 2916-E Ainaola Dr., Hilo, HI 96720. 808/959–3488 or 808/932–1121.

Kalani Honua—This 20-acre oceanfront resort has many faces: It's a Japanese spa; an equestrian center; a retreat with dance, language, yoga, and arts programs; and offers other activities. Accommodations are in five cedar lodges. Some rooms share baths. The resort is near the Kalapana black sand beach and the lava fields. Facilities include a pool, stables, and health spa. Inexpensive. P.O. Box 4500, Kalapana, HI 96778. 808/965–7828.

Kilauea Lodge—This four-room lodge is one of the more romantic retreats on the island. Located in a forest a mile outside of Volcanoes National Park, the lodge offers three rooms decorated with Hawaiian motifs and one in Oriental style. Each room has a fireplace and bath. Inexpensive (and a great country breakfast is included). P.O. Box 116, Volcano Village, HI 96785. 808/967-7366.

My Island Bed and Breakfast—This century-old house, the oldest in Volcano, has three rooms and one studio apartment in the house and two more studio apartments in another building. The rooms are spacious. The house was built by the Lyman missionary family. Inexpensive. P.O. Box 100, Volcano, HI 96785. 808/967-7216.

Volcano House—This lodge on the edge of the Kilauea volcano is Hawaii's oldest hotel. It offers 38 simply furnished but comfortable rooms, some with a fantastic view of the crater. Inexpensive. P.O. Box 53, Hawaii Volcanoes National Park, HI 96718-0053. 808/967-7321.

On the Kona and Kohala Coasts:

Aston Royal Sea Cliff—This 150-unit condominium resort offers spacious and beautifully furnished rooms on seven acres on the coast. The grounds are lovely, and facilities include two pools, hot tub, sauna, health club, and tennis courts. Expensive. 75-6040 Alii Dr., Kailua-Kona, HI 96740. 808/329-8021 or 800/922-7866.

Aston Shore at Waikoloa—These plush villas offer luxurious one- and two-bedroom suites with full kitchens, large patios, and beautiful landscaping (waterfalls and lagoons). Facilities include a pool, hot tub, golf, tennis, and horseback riding. Expensive. Star Rt. 5200-A, Waikoloa, HI 96743. 808/885-5001 or 800/922-7866.

Hotel King Kamehameha—Located next to the waterfront in Kailua-Kona and on the former grounds of the king's palace, this downtown, 460-room, twin-tower resort offers a small white sand beach, displays of Hawaiian art, and tours of the restored palace compound. The rooms are not exceptional, but the location can't be beat if you want to be near the waterfront and in the city. Moderate. 75-5660 Palani Rd., Kailua-Kona, HI 96740. 808/329-2911 or 800/227-4700.

THE ORIGIN OF THE LUAU

Considered by many to be an ancient part of Hawaii's culture, luaus are really a fairly recent form of feasting in the islands. The Hawaiian word *lu'au* literally means a dish of young taro (a sweet potato-like vegetable) tops, cooked with coconut milk, chicken, and seafood. The word wasn't associated with a feast until 1856, when the *Pacific Commercial Advertiser* newspaper used it to describe a feast that until then was called a *pa'ina.*

Since then, entertaining in the islands has never been the same. Luaus are characterized by a main course of a whole pig, roasted in an *imu,* or underground pit lined with lava rocks, and other dishes including the taro tops, poi, fish, vegetables, and meats and fish.

In some of the quiet communities and islands, luaus are like potluck dinners held to celebrate a birth, wedding, anniversary, or homecoming. While these luaus are closed to outsiders, the next best alternatives are those thrown occasionally by island churches to raise funds for their projects. Look in the local papers for listings of these events.

The luaus at the big resorts, hotels, and nightspots are lavish affairs. While they follow the traditional menu—pig roasted in imu, served with poi—these luaus are more like all-you-can-eat buffets with a floor show. Still, don't miss them. They are a touching reminder of life on the islands a century ago.

Hyatt Regency at Waikoloa—Words fail us. This is a resort masquerading as a theme park. Or is it a theme park with rooms? The huge (1,241 rooms in three buildings) resort offers something for everyone: a series of lagoons used for decoration and for transportation by the boats that shuttle endlessly around the resort; a monorail, looking much like the one in Disneyland; eight

Removing the roast pig from the imu pit signals the start of the luau. *(Photo courtesy of Barbara Radin-Fox)*

restaurants, each with a different theme; island with exotic animals; three huge outdoor pools and one indoor; a river lagoon for swimming; swim-with-the-dolphins program; water sports and sunbathing on its sand beach, which isn't on the sea; numerous shops; waterfalls; eight tennis courts; health spa; racquetball, and a golf course. Throughout all this are many beautiful places— gardens, walks, bridges, and more. It's a bit overwhelming, but a big hit with families with young children and young honeymooners. Even if you don't stay here you must visit it. Despite its size, this Hyatt does a remarkable job of controlling the flow of guests throughout the complex. We wish all the megaresorts could do as well. Expensive. One Waikoloa Beach Resort, Kohala Coast, HI 96734. 808/885–1234 or 800/228–9000.

Kanaloa at Kona—Very large one- to three-bedroom condominium apartments make this 118-unit resort a place for those who want lots of living space. The apartments are very nicely furnished. The oceanfront suites have private jacuzzis. Facilities include three pools and tennis courts. Expensive. 78261 Manukai St., Kailua-Kona, HI 96740. 808/322–2272 or 800/367–6046.

Keauhou Resort—The 48 condo apartments set amid five acres of lush gardens are spacious and comfortable. Facilities include a golf course, two pools, and some beautiful gardens. Expensive. 78-7039 Kamehameha III Rd., Kailua-Kona, HI 96740. 808/322–9122 or 800/367–5286.

Kona Coast Resort—The 68 rooms in this beautiful 12-acre resort are stylish and have every amenity and gadget any traveler would ever need (hair dryers, microwaves, washers, and dryers). The rooms are spacious and very nicely furnished, and have beautiful views of the ocean and golf course. Facilities include pool and spa. Expensive. 78-6842 Alii Dr., Kailua-Kona, HI 96740. 808/324–1721 or 800/367–8047.

Kona Hilton Beach and Tennis Resort—Located just south of Kailua-Kona's waterfront, this 542-room resort offers some striking views of the ocean. The rooms are spacious and comfortably furnished but not exceptional. The best views are to be found from the oceanfront rooms in the Beach Building.

Facilities include a pool and four tennis courts. Expensive. P.O. Box 1179, Kailua-Kona, HI 96745. 808/329-3111 or 800/452-4411.

Kona Village Resort—This resort may be the ultimate in Polynesian privacy. It returns you to the lifestyle of yesteryear when couples lived in thatched *hales* (houses) next to the sea. The 125 hales are scattered around the shoreline, and offer a lot of privacy along with the almost-modern (no TV, telephone, or radio) accommodations. Facilities include the nice beach, tennis, diving and sailing school, and pool. Pure bliss! Expensive. P.O. Box 1299, Kaupulehu-Kona, HI 96745. 808/325-5555 or 800/367-5290.

Manago Hotel—Set in the middle of Kona coffee country, this 74-year-old hotel offers striking views of the coastline below, 64 comfortable rooms (including a Japanese-style suite), and great value. Some rooms share a bath. Expensive. P.O. Box 145, Captain Cook, HI 96704. 808/323-2642.

Mauna Kea Beach Resort—This is the resort that set standards for other super luxury resorts to follow. Built in 1965 by Laurance Rockefeller, this fabulous resort has changed owners several times but still offers the best white sand beach on the Big Island; striking Polynesian, Asian, and African art in its hallways and public areas; meticulous service; dramatic landscaping; paths made for romantic moonlit walks; and a style of elegance rarely found these days. The downside is that the 1960s-style rooms are small, and the tropical furnishings seem out of the same era. The biggest rooms are in the Ocean View addition. Facilities include a Robert Trent Jones, Sr., golf course, pool, water sports, 13 tennis courts, fitness center, exercise trails, and education programs. Expensive. P.O. Box 218, Kamuela, HI 96743. 808/882-7222 or 800/228-3000.

Mauna Lani Bay Hotel—The most luxurious resort on the island, this fantastic hotel excels in every way: all the rooms are lovely and spacious, and all offer wonderful views of the ocean; there are three miles of shoreline, including white sand beaches (particularly the one reached by walking south about a quarter-mile) that offer fine swimming and nice snorkeling; the landscaping is sensational; and the series of ancient spring- and ocean-fed fish pools in the black lava on the grounds offer beauty as well as a continuing education on marine life. In the pools are turtles, dog sharks, exotic and colorful tropical fish, and other strange creatures. This resort is so complete, so wonderful that even the open-air atrium is romantic. It's filled with coconut palms, waterfalls, fish ponds, and gardens—all tastefully lighted at night. If money is no obstacle, check into one of the five private bungalows overlooking their own stretch of fish ponds and beach. For only $2,500 a night, you get a beautiful, spacious, two-bedroom bungalow furnished with tables and chairs, and walls made from Hawaii's striking koa wood. Outside is a private patio, pool, and jacuzzi. You can do the cooking yourself or have the staff of 26 do it (or anything else) for you. Facilities include a golf course, pool, ten tennis courts, spa, walking trails, and educational programs. Don't miss the bungalow tours offered almost daily, although you may turn green with envy. Expensive. P.O. Box 4000, Kawaihae, HI 96743. 808/885–6622 or 800/356–6652.

Mauna Lani Point Condominiums—A short walk away from the Mauna Lani Bay Resort, this 116-unit complex is popular with those who need kitchen and living space. The villas are spacious and fully equipped. Guests share all the facilities of the Mauna Lani Bay Hotel. Expensive. Two Kaniku Dr., Kohala Coast, HI 96743. 808/885–5022 or 800/642–6284.

Ritz-Carlton—This 542-room resort is the Big Island's newest, and is blending the high standards and expectations accompany the Ritz-Carlton name with a tropical environment. Surprisingly, it works. The rooms are spacious, and have the dark wood furnishings familiar to devotees of this hotel group. Facilities include a pool, small beach, 11 tennis courts, golf course, fitness center, walking and jogging trails, and a superb location between the Mauna Lani Bay Hotel and the Mauna Kea Beach Hotel. Expensive. One N. Kaniku Dr., Kohala Coast, HI 96743. 808/885–2000.

Royal Waikoloan—Recently remodeled, this 523-room resort offers ocean views, private lanais, and a small white sand beach. The rooms are comfortable and nicely furnished. The resort is next to some royal fish ponds, and its decor emphasizes Hawaiian art. Facilities include two golf courses, a pool, six tennis courts, and walking trails. Expensive. Box 5000, Waikoloa Rd., Kohala Coast, HI 96743. 808/921–9700.

Around Waimea:

Kamuela Inn—This attractive and cozy 21-room country inn offers comfortable rooms in a lush setting. The penthouse suite has a fireplace, lanai, and kitchen. All rooms have private baths. Expensive (includes breakfast). P.O. Box 1994, Kamuela, HI 96743. 808/885–4243.

Parker Ranch Lodge—This rustic, 20-room lodge offers simple accommodations on the ranch and a sense of adventure. Inexpensive. P.O. Box 458, Kamuela, HI 96743. 808/885–4100.

Two B&B reservation services can offer your accommodations in private homes and cottages. Call Bed & Breakfast-Hawaii at 800/657-7832, Bed & Breakfast Honolulu (statewide listings) at 800/288-4666, ext. 351, or Bed & Breakfast Pacific-Hawaii at 808/254-5030.

Where to Dine

The better restaurants on the islands are usually in the finest resorts. There are two drawbacks to this situation—dress codes and (usually) high costs—and only one advantage—convenience, if you are staying in that resort.

However, for those willing to venture outside their resort or hotel, some special dining rooms await. Always make reservations and always ask about the dress code.

The price categories for restaurants, for two persons for dinner, excluding wine, tips, and taxes, are:

Expensive—More than $75.
Moderate—$25 to $75.
Inexpensive—Less than $25.

Our Favorites in and Around Hilo:

Fuji—This comfortable and casual restaurant is a favorite of Hilo's Japanese community, who praise the sashimi, tempura, and stir-fry chicken and steak. The room is a bit noisy, but Fuji is worth it. Inexpensive. 142 Kinoole St. (in the Hilo Hotel), Hilo. 808/961-3733.

Harrington's—This waterfront dining room serves American standbys: steak and seafood. Stick to the fish dishes, which are sensational. Moderate. 135 Kalanianaole St., Hilo. 808/961-4966.

KK TEI—Another local hangout, this restaurant serves Japanese and American fare. It's a bargain for the amount of food served and the excellent quality. Inexpensive. 1550 Kamehameha Ave., Hilo. 808/961-3791.

Roussel's—This is a real surprise: a Cajun restaurant, and one that is great; the two brothers who own it are from Louisiana. Stick to the Cajun dishes: creole shrimp, Trout Alexander, and other seafood dishes. Moderate. 60 Keawe St., Hilo. 808/935-5111.

Tex Drive Inn—It's not very romantic, and it sure isn't elegant, but it does serve fantastic malasadas—those yeasty dumplings that are deep-fried and then rolled in sugar. Inexpensive. Highway 19, Honokaa (no phone).

Uncle Billy's—This is a fun spot, one decorated with a grass roof and the usual assortment of batik, bamboo, and wooden items. The chicken and seafood dishes are outstanding. Moderate. 87 Banyan Dr. (In the Hilo Bay Hotel), Hilo. 808/935-0861.

Our Favorites on the Kona and Kohala Coasts:

Aloha Cafe—Casual and funky, this cafe is better for breakfast than for dinner. Fresh pastries, great corn bread, outstanding brownies, tasty omelets and Kona coffee are served in this restaurant located in what once was the historic Aloha Theater. Inexpensive. On Highway 11 in Kainaliu. 808/329-3822.

La Bourgogne—It's small, but this French country restaurant serves excellent lamb, veal, and other classics. Expensive. Kuakini Plaza, on Highway 11. 808/329-6711.

Harrington's—This casual but pleasant restaurant shares the same menu and ownership as the original in Hilo. Even the waterfront setting—this time at the Kawaihae Harbor—is the same. The menu features American standbys: pasta, steak, and seafood. Stick to the local fish dishes, which are sensational. Moderate. Mahukona Highway and Wharf Rd., Kawaihae. 808/882-7997.

Hyatt Regency Waikoloa—Of the eight theme restaurants in the fantasy resort, the best is Donatello's, where classic Italian and light seafood dishes, as well as pizzas made to order, are served. The room is huge (340 seats) though, and can be noisy. Moderate. 808/885-1234.

Kona Ranch House—This isn't a beautiful restaurant, but it does have excellent food. You have a choice of two decors—plain cafe or Hawaii plantation—and one menu serving excellent barbecue and fresh local fish. Inexpensive. 75-5653 Olioli St., Kailua-Kona. 808/329-7061.

Manago Restaurant—This casual restaurant serves some of the finest fish dishes. Try the ahi, or the mahimahi, and don't miss the seaweed. Inexpensive. Located in the Manago Hotel in Captain Cook. 808/329-9998.

Mauna Kea Beach Resort—This excellent resort has superb restaurants. Try the Batik Room for Indonesian, Thai, and continental dishes, or The Pavilion for continental cuisine and grilled meats. Both are expensive. 808/882-7222.

Mauna Lani Bay Hotel—Three dining rooms at the fabulous resort are worth visiting. For Pacific Rim cuisine served in a casual open-air spot, try the CanoeHouse. The food is fabulous—the seafood, sushi, and sashimi are heavenly. Care must be taken, for the appetizers are so good and the servings so large that you can make a meal out of just them. Le Soleil serves classic French dishes in a very elegant setting. The Gallery, winner of Travel/

Holiday awards, at the racquet club serves excellent seafood, accented with such local touches as seaweed and passion fruit. All three are expensive. Call 808/885-7777 for The Gallery, 808/885-6622 for CanoeHouse or Le Soleil.

Sibu Cafe—An informal spot in Kailua-Kona serving excellent Indonesian food. Stick to the chicken or vegetarian dishes. Inexpensive. Banyan Court, Alii Dr., Kailua-Kona. 808/329-1112.

Our Favorites on the North Shore and Near Waimea:

Bread Depot—It's a bakery, and you will have to come early for the famed cinnamon rolls. Stick around for the clam chowder, which may be the island's finest. Inexpensive. Opelo Plaza, Highway 19, Waimea. 808/885-6354.

Bree Garden—The chef once worked at the Mauna Kea resort. Now Bernd Bree dishes up French, Vietnamese, and an eclectic assortment of other cuisines at his lovely restaurant, which is built around a lovely banyan tree. Moderate. 64-5188 Kinohou St., Kamuela. 808/885-4736.

Don's Family Deli—There isn't much on the northern tip of the Big Island, so Don's, a vegetarian spot, is a welcome surprise. The lasagna, quiche, and bean soup are wonderful. Inexpensive. In Kapaau, across from the statue of King Kamehameha. 808/889-5822.

Edelweiss—This is a casual restaurant, but the European nouvelle dishes are outstanding. Go early for dinner to avoid a wait. Inexpensive. On Highway 19 in Kamuela/Waimea. 808/885-6800.

Merriman's—This restaurant serves up regional cuisine, which means Parker Ranch beef and seafood. Both are outstanding, as is the Hawaiian art decor. Moderate. Opelo Plaza, Highway 19, Waimea. 808/885-6822.

Luaus and Other Nightlife

The best luau on the island is at the Kona Villa Resort. It's held on Fridays and costs about $45. Call 808/325-5555. For other luaus, try the Mauna Kea Beach Resort, which has a luau feast every Tuesday. It's $29 for hotel guests, $50 for nonguests. Call 808/882-7222. The Hotel King Kamehameha holds luaus on Tuesdays, Thursdays, and Sundays. The cost is $36 for adults, $22 for children under 13. Call 808/329-2911. The Hyatt Regency Waikoloa holds its "Legends of Polynesia" dinner buffet and show on Tuesdays and Fridays. The dinner is $49 for adults, $29 for children 5-12. For cocktails only, the price is $26 for adults, $17 for minors. Call 808/885-1234.

For nightlife, the major hotels have music and dancing most nights. The liveliest spot is the Spats Disco at the Hyatt Regency Waikoloa. Otherwise, it's a very quiet island, despite its size.

The beach scene at the Stouffer Waiohai Beach Resort on Kauai.
(Photo courtesy of Sheila Donnelly & Associates)

CHAPTER 2

Kauai: The Garden Island

*P*aradise is the word that first and frequently comes to mind when visiting Kauai. This small island is so green, so lush with colorful flowers and exotic vegetation, that it is the island that comes closest to fulfilling any dreams of a garden of Eden. (This fact has not escaped Hollywood producers; scenes from "South Pacific," "Raiders of the Lost Ark," and the TV miniseries "The Thorn Birds" were filmed here.)

Rural and yet sophisticated, Kauai is a charming island whose attractions lie both inside in its fine galleries, resorts, and towns and outside in the beautiful countryside. Fourth-largest and the oldest of the islands, Kauai was formed by the volcano Waialeale, whose summit reaches 5,243 feet above sea level. Waialeale is just the most visible part of the striking scenery found here. Kauai has a vast canyon that is truly grand, a northern coast sculpted by wind and water into the most dramatic scenery in all the islands, and a mountainous interior that gets more than 500 inches of rain a year, siring scores of rushing rivers and waterfalls.

Touring Kauai is simple. The island is a rough oval, covering 548 square miles. The airport is on the southeast shore just outside the main town of Lihue. From Lihue the road heads north along the east coast and then curves west around the volcano Waialeale to the north shore, passing through the resort areas of Wailua, Kapaa, and Hanalei. This is the wet and lush side of the island, a region with fantastic plants and flowers, mighty waterfalls, and myths.

The legends say that the hula dance was created in the village of Haena. Perhaps so, but another myth, one shrouded in mystery but still visible in mysterious stoneworks, is the legend of the menehune. The menehune, so the legend goes, were tiny people, and may have come to the islands before the Polynesians. These people were master stonebuilders who worked only at night.

Little more is known about them, for they have vanished into history. The stone walls and ditches remain, though, and you can see them even today.

South from Lihue, the road follows the coast, passing the resort area of Poipu Beach and the Waimea Canyon region before turning north and ending at the impenetrable Na Pali Coast, an area as beautiful as it is rugged. The southern coast is drier than the northern and eastern shores, but this is relative. Passing showers are common, with the droplets often so tiny that the showers are more like a whirling mist. The rain is so light that many people don't bother to get an umbrella.

Kauai can be seen in a few days, but the beauty of the island will make you want to linger far longer. Lihue and the smaller villages on Kauai are colorful and interesting places that retain the heritage of their plantation and seafaring pasts amid the sprawl of new development. In these hamlets are numerous galleries and shops selling the creations of Kauai's artists and craftspersons. Surrounding all these man-made attractions is a world of splendor saturated with every possible hue of green, the color of paradise.

Lihue and the Road North

Lihue is a once-small plantation town caught up in both the ups and downs that a fast-growing population and development boom brings. Shopping centers, familiar fast-food restaurants, and small housing developments seem to overwhelm the town.

Start a tour of old Lihue on Rice Street, the main commercial road in the city. The Kauai Museum at 4428 Rice Street occupies two buildings that exhibit the island's heritage and history. The William Hyde Rice Building shows short films of aerial views of the island's magnificent scenery and exhibits that trace the island's history from its volcanic birth through the nineteenth century. The adjacent Albert Spencer Wilcox Building, Lihue's former library, is a showcase of Hawaiiana and sells some fine artwork from the island, Nihau, and Polynesia. The museum is

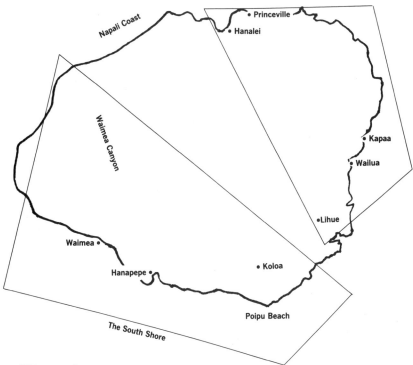

Napali Coast

Princeville

Hanalei

Waimea Canyon

Kapaa

Wailua

Lihue

Waimea

Koloa

Hanapepe

Poipu Beach

The South Shore

Kauai

open weekdays from 9:00 AM–4:30 PM, Saturdays from 9:00 AM–1:00 PM.

A block east of the museum is Umi Street. At 3016 Umi Street you will find the Hawaii Visitors' Bureau. There you can get maps, brochures, and other information about current activities on Kauai and other islands.

Continue east on Rice Street to Waapa Road and turn right and drive to Nawiliwili, the big port on the island. There isn't much to see here, unless you like commercial and tour ships, but there is a fine beach in the cove, Kalapaki Beach, which sits next to the enormous Westin Kauai resort.

Continue on Waapa Road and turn right on Highway 58. This area of Kauai was once part of a vast sugar cane plantation, and the Grove Farm Homestead on this road is a living museum of early plantation life. Beyond the homestead is the Menehune Garden, a living-history park where ancient island music, dances, and rituals are performed in a lovely garden setting. A bit farther on Highway 58, at the lookout on Niumalu Road just off the highway, is the Menehune Fish Pond. The 900-foot-long stone walls hold a fish pond and are said to have been built by the menehune for a royal couple. The old tale adds that the twin stone pillars on the mountainside above are that royal couple, who spied on the tiny people at work and paid the price by being turned into stone. The ponds are used to raise mullet today.

Drive north again on Highway 58 and turn right on Highway 50, which takes you into Lihue again and then turn north on Highway 56. This road leads all the way to the northern coast, where it ends in the rugged and impassable Na Pali region. It's a full day's drive, longer if you want to take part in some of the boat tours that are offered along the way. If that is your plan, you should consider making reservations for overnight accommodations in the Princeville area, near the north end of the road.

From Lihue, take Highway 56 north to Highway 538. This small rural road takes you four miles through fields of sugarcane to an overlook that gives you a view of the beautiful Wailua Falls. The falls were used for the opening sequence of the old "Fantasy Island" television series.

Return to Highway 56 and drive north again. This road

passes by a number of resorts and through some of the island's most colorful villages. In Wailua, you will find evidence of some of the island's oldest settlements. Turn left on Highway 580, a road that once was a highway for kings. Commoners were not allowed to walk it. On this route just off the main road is a platform of rocks, the Pohaku Ho'Ohanau, a sacred place where sacrifices were made to please the gods.

A mile farther on Highway 580 is Opaekaa Falls, another lovely waterfall that is quite striking. Across from the falls is Kamokila Hawaiian Village, a restored village of grass huts, exhibits, and demonstrations. The village is a bit touristy, but interesting nonetheless.

Return again to Highway 56 and continue north to Wailua Marina, where you can catch a boat ride up the Wailua River to the Fern Grotto. The grotto is a massive lava cavern, whose face is covered with huge ferns and other plants. It's a very picturesque place, one of such beauty that hundreds of weddings are performed there each year. The boats leave on the half hour. The trips take one hour, and include entertainment on the way. The cost is about $9 per person. Behind the marina is Smith's Tropical Paradise, 31 acres of lovely tropical gardens and lagoons and recreated Polynesian villages.

Travel north again on Highway 56 to Lydgate State Park, a coconut grove that was a place of refuge for wrongdoers. If the lawbreaker reached the grove, island law once held, he was safe from the wrath of the king. The beach at the park is nice for beachcombing and swimming, depending on the wind and size of the waves.

The next stop on Highway 56 is Waipouli, whose main attraction is the Coconut Marketplace, a collection of 70 shops that sell everything. If you are lucky, you will stop there when demonstrations of Hawaiian crafts, music, or hula take place.

Beyond Waipouli is Kapaa, another town being changed by development. Numerous small shopping malls compete with the shops and galleries in the older buildings. Among the better shops are Classical Glass, at 4523 Nui Street, for sales of glass art; Kauai Crafts in Progress, 1384 Kuhio Highway (Highway 56); Lady

ISLANDS OF THE STARS

Hawaii's beautiful landscape has attracted movie makers ever since Thomas Edison took the first films of the islands in 1898. More than 100 English and Japanese language films have been filmed all or in part in the islands. And that total doesn't include the more than 50 television shows, films, and miniseries filmed on the islands.

Many of these efforts are certainly forgettable. These include movies like "She Gods of Shark Reef" (1958) and "Hot Lips and Inner Tubes" (1976), as well as such classic TV specials as "Maui Jail Break" (1960), "The Wally Amos Happiness Hour" (1987), and "The New Gidget" (1987).

Here is a critics' guide to the best of Hawaii's films:

Curly Top, with Shirley Temple (1935); *Pagan Love Song*, with Esther Williams and Howard Kiel (1950); *From Here to Eternity*, with Montgomery Clift, Frank Sinatra, Burt Lancaster, and Deborah Kerr (1953); *Miss Sadie Thompson*, with Rita Hayworth and Jose Ferrer (1954); *Mr. Roberts*, with Henry Fonda, Jack Lemmon, and James Cagney (1955); *The Revolt of Mamie*

Jane's Company, 3-4684 Kuhio Highway, and Nighten' Gales, 4-1312 Kuhio Highway, all of which sell some fine crafts.

After Kapaa, the distance between the towns begins to grow as the scenery becomes more lush, more green. Seven miles north is Anahola, a small, unremarkable place whose main attraction is the fine beach at Anahola Beach Park.

A few miles farther is Kilauea, another plantation town with some interesting old homes and stores and the unusual St. Sylvester's Catholic Church. The church is in the shape of an octagon and is decorated inside with Jean Charlot frescoes.

Take the nearby Kolo Road down to the Kilauea Lighthouse and a seaside bluff popular with red-footed boobies and other rare seabirds. A visitors' center at the Kilauea Wildlife Refuge offers exhibits and information on the birds. Trails lead from the center into the 129-acre park.

Stover, with Jane Russell and Richard Egan (1956); *South Pacific*, with Rossano Brazzi and Mitzi Gaynor (1958); *Blue Hawaii*, with Elvis Presley (1961); *Hawaii*, with Julie Andrews and Max von Sydow (1966); *Papillon*, with Dustin Hoffman (1973); *King Kong*, with Jessica Lange (1976); *10*, with Bo Derek and Dudley Moore (1979); *Raiders of the Lost Ark*, with Harrison Ford (1980); and *Joe Versus the Volcano*, with Tom Hanks (1989).

A number of popular television series were based in Hawaii. "Adventures in Paradise" (1959–62), "Hawaiian Eye" (1959–63), "Hawaii Five-O" (1968–80), "Magnum P.I." (1980–88), and "Jake and the Fatman" (1988–90) are the longest running of the series. Among the miniseries filmed in the islands, "From Here to Eternity" (1978–79), "The Thorn Birds" (1982), "Blood and Orchids" (1985), and "War and Remembrance" (1987) were the most successful.

More than 40 hit television comedy, drama, and talk shows have filmed some episodes in Hawaii. These include "The Lucille Ball Show," "China Beach," "Fantasy Island," "Arthur Godfrey Show," "Hart to Hart," "Murder She Wrote," "Jack Parr Show," "Tour of Duty," "Dr. Who," and "The Young and the Restless."

Beyond Kilauea is the Kalihiwai Valley Overlook, a magnificent valley with yet another beautiful waterfall. You can see the valley from the overlook near mile marker 25 on Highway 56.

The road curves around the northern shore by now, and the next stop is the Princeville area of resorts, shopping centers, and golf courses. Across from the shops is the Hanalei Valley Overlook.

Beyond these attractions, across a one-lane bridge, is Hanalei, a pleasant town caught in a time warp. The architecture is from the late nineteenth and early twentieth centuries. The Waioli Mission was built in 1836, and the quaint, green Waioli Hui'ia Church was erected in 1912. The Hanalei Museum, located in a plantation cottage, offers exhibits on the town's past.

Hanalei also has a wonderful beach, and its proximity to the spectacular Na Pali Coast makes it the headquarters for the Zodiac Boat Tours of that area.

Continue on Highway 56 to the marked turnoff for Lumahai Beach, a mile-long strand of white sand that was used in the movie "South Pacific." The beach's backdrop of rugged, green cliffs, black lava boulders, and vegetation makes it a sensational place for a swim. A bit farther on Highway 56 is Tunnels Beach, another nice spot where the boat tours start.

At road's end is another attraction, a place of myth, mystery and perhaps even a bit of magic. At Ke'e State Beach Park, a lovely area with a great view of the Na Pali Coast, is a path leading from the shore to a meadow with a stone platform called the Lohiau's Dance Pavilion.

On those rocks, island folklore holds, Laka, the goddess of hula, did her dancing. For Hawaiians, this is a sacred place, not a forum of entertainment. Laka was an important goddess, one whose powers and spiritual influence remain strong even today. The proof lies on the altar, where offerings of flowers, fruits, and other items are donated by other dancers of the hula.

The South Shore

The southern shore of Kauai is a region of sugarcane plantations and picturesque mill towns, grand resorts, and scenery more suited to the desert of the Southwest than to a Pacific island.

Just west of Lihue on Highway 50 is Kilohana Plantation, a 35-acre estate that is home to the Wilcox House. The grand house has been restored to look as it did in 1935, when it was built. It is a showplace of Hawaiian and South Pacific artifacts. Elsewhere on the plantation are restored buildings now housing shops and a restaurant. Carriage rides are also offered on the grounds.

West of Kilohana, Highway 50 passes through a lush landscape of eucalyptus trees, wild ginger, and other exotic flora. Beyond the fields on both sides of the road are magnificent, rugged bluffs covered with a thick quilt of green.

Drive west to Highway 520 and turn south toward Koloa. This first stretch of Highway 520 leads into a tunnel formed by the eucalyptus trees on both sides of the road.

Koloa is a historic sugar mill town that is now shaded with massive banyan trees and lined with a nice collection of shops and restaurants clustered among the banyans at the intersection of highways 520 and 530.

Koloa was the island's first sugar plantation town, built in 1835 around the mill that processed the plantation crops. All that remains of the original mill is the stone chimney at the entrance to the town.

The shops here are worth a visit. For clothing and sportswear, visit The Sand People, Nona Koloa, and Paradise Clothing. The Kahana Ki'i Gallery, Indo-Pacific Trading Company, Island Images Fine Art, and Return to Paradise sell fine gifts, jewelry, and craft items. This small town is also the place to book helicopter and boat tours, dive and snorkel trips, and other adventures.

Continue south on Highway 520 to Poipu Road and turn left to visit the beautiful resorts found along the shore. Here you will find such fine resorts as the Stouffer Waiohai, Sheraton Kauai, and Kiahuna Plantation, as well as the Kiahuna Shopping Village. The latter is a nicely landscaped open-air mall, featuring fine shops, an excellent bakery, and a few lower-priced restaurants.

For shopping, visit the Black Pearl Collection, Golden Nugget, and the Tideline Gallery for jewelry; the Elephant Walk and South Pacific Collection for art and gifts, and the Land and Sea Leathers for fine leather goods. The Whaler's General Store is the best place by far for buying shell leis and snorkeling equipment. We bought these items for far less than we would have paid elsewhere on the island. We particularly enjoyed the freshly baked cinnamon rolls at the Garden Isle Bake Shoppe, although we and others had to rise early to get them before the shop sold out.

Across the road is the Kiahuna Plantation Resort and Gardens. The estate is listed in *Great Gardens of America* because it has more than 4,000 varieties of plants, orchids, and other exotic flora. It is open daily, with tours starting at 10:00 AM.

For swimming, Poipu Road leads to Poipu Beach Park, where the beach is a small crescent of sand. Return west on Poipu Road to the turnoff for Kukuiula Bay and Spouting Horn. The bay is a picturesque small harbor and water sports center. A tiny beach is available, but most swimmers walk across the lava rocks to the water. Beyond the condos and houses on the bay is another park where the Lawai Road ends. The Spouting Horn is a shoreline lava tunnel that, when the surf hits it just right, sends a geyser of water into the air and makes a moaning sound. Legend has it that the sound is the cry of a giant lizard trapped within the earth.

The park here is also home to a score of vendors selling a wide variety of trinkets, necklaces, jewelry, and gifts. The prices on most items are very good.

The island seen offshore is Nihau, the Forbidden Island. Return again through Kukuiula Bay to Highway 530 and turn north for a scenic drive through the bucolic Lawai Valley. There isn't much development along this road. One attraction is the Pacific Tropical Botanical Garden, a 186-acre research plantation and 100-acre estate garden with more than 6,000 species of plants, including more than 500 different palms, 50 varieties of bananas, and more than 100 diverse coral trees. Two-hour tours of the gardens are conducted by expert guides at 9:00 AM and 1:00 PM weekdays, 9:00 AM Saturdays and 1:00 PM Sundays. (Reservations for the tours are a must and should be made in advance of your trip. The cost is about $15; call 808/332–7361.)

Where Highway 530 meets Highway 50 is the town of Kalaheo and the Kukuiolono Park, a preserve offering Japanese gardens, exhibits of Hawaiian artifacts, and outstanding views of the coast. Farther west on Highway 50 is the Hanapepe Valley

Overlook on your right. The scenery is beautiful and historic, for the valley was where Kauai's last battle between King Kamehameha and the local ruler, King Kaumualii, took place.

Farther down the road you come to Hanapepe, which a local billboard describes as "The Biggest Little Town on Kauai." The town is colorful, though shabby. Hanapepe Road was used as a street scene in the television miniseries "The Thorn Birds." The tired frame buildings once housed taverns and brothels catering to the sailors from the port. The street is changing, though, and several of these houses now hold very nice art galleries, artists' studios, and boutiques.

West of town is another historic attraction, the ruins of Fort Elizabeth. The stone fort, marked by the Hawaiian warrior roadside sign, was built of stone in 1816 by Imperial Russian officials who tried to conquer the island for the czar. The ruins are crumbling and overgrown, but offer some spectacular views of the coast.

Take Highway 50 across the Waimea River, where there are two attractions, one a mystery and the other a wonder of nature. Menehune Road, the first right turn west of the river, takes you 2.5 miles up the valley to the Menehune Ditch, a meticulously engineered channel credited by archeologists to the mysterious little people.

Waimea, the town back on Highway 50, is the commercial center of the west side of the island. Waimea was the village that welcomed English explorer Captain James Cook to the islands in 1778, and two generations later saw the arrival of the first missionaries to Hawaii. The Waimea Hawaiian and Foreign Church, a timber and limestone structure, was built in 1846 by those first missionaries. It and other old churches and general stores line the streets of the quaint town.

The wonder of nature at this end of the island is the Waimea Canyon State Park, labeled "The Grand Canyon of the Pacific." And it truly is a grand sight.

Two roads lead into the park. From the small town of Kekaha, Kokee Road climbs steeply into the park. From Waimea,

Highway 550 leads into the park and, while steep, is an easier drive than the Kokee Road.

Whichever way you take leads you to a point a few miles inland where the two roads merge and continue the climb up into first Waimea Canyon State Park and then Kokee State Park. Marked overlooks with parking areas offer spectacular views of the gorge, which reaches depths of 3,600 feet.

The canyon is a landscape painted with greens, deep reds, and solid blacks. Hiking trails, some with the plants identified along the way, wind throughout the park, though many of the walks can be difficult. The weather on the high canyon rim is very changeable. During the drive up you can pass through mist to sunshine to rain and then to a downpour before emerging into sunshine again.

In the Kokee State Park is the Kokee Museum, the park headquarters, and the Kokee Lodge. The museum has a nice collection of nature exhibits, the park headquarters has many maps on the hiking trails and other information, and the lodge is a restaurant that offers some spectacular views of the Na Pali coast along with fine food.

At road's end is the Kalalau Lookout, situated some 4,120 feet above the seashore below. From this perch, the beauty of the canyon comes alive. All the waterfalls, earthen colors, and thic k vegetation blend into a kaleidoscope of nature.

For More Information

Kauai's airports, hotels, and rental car companies have a wide variety of maps, driving guides, brochures, current-events magazines, and other publications. They are very helpful for touring the island.

The Lihue Airport Visitor Information Center (808/246–1440); the Hawaii Visitors' Bureau (3016 Umi St., Lihue Plaza, Suite 207, Lihue, HI 96766, 808/245–3971); and the Kauai Visitor Center in the Coconut Plantation Market in Waipouli (808/822–0987) are great sources of information.

NIHAU: THE FORBIDDEN ISLAND

Nihau, for so long an island closed to outsiders, is opening its doors a crack. A very tiny crack.

The 46,000-acre island 17 miles off the western coast of Kauai is an anachronism, a place where time seems to have stopped in the late 1800s. Only close relatives of the 225 residents and an occasional doctor or official are allowed by the Robinson family, who owns the island, to visit Nihau.

The closing of the island began in 1864, when King Kamehameha V sold it for $10,000 to Elizabeth Sinclair, the daughter of a prosperous Scottish merchant. She and her children made the island a sheep and cattle ranch and hired the island's residents as employees.

The Sinclairs soon moved from Nihau to Kauai, and Mrs. Sinclair decided, for reasons still unclear, to preserve the old ways of Hawaiian life on the island of Nihau. That meant keeping the residents apart from the advances of the twentieth century. There are no telephones, televisions, and almost no cars. The only electricity is in the Robinson homestead.

The residents, most of whom are pure-blooded Hawaiians, live and work on the ranch, and have a thriving sideline of making the beautiful and highly prized Nihau shell leis. The leis are made from the tiny, colorful shells that are harvested every October on the island beaches.

The Robinsons recently lowered the barriers to the outside world a bit, using their emergency helicopter to fly tourists on a sightseeing tour of the western coastline. The helicopter makes two landings: one at a sunken volcanic crater and the second at a cliff overlooking a beach. Going off on your own, though, is still forbidden. The decision to admit tourists, even on such a restricted basis, was made to help subsidize the costs of the helicopter. If you want to see the forbidden island, call Nihau Helicopters at 808/338–1234. The cost starts at $135 per person.

Festivals

Captain Cook Festival—Three days of canoe races, a fair, and a reenactment of the explorer's landing. February.

Cherry Blossom Festival—A celebration of Japanese culture and heritage, with music, dance, and food featured. Late February/early March.

Buddha Day—A pageant of flowers with parades and other activities. April.

Lei Day—Celebration of the flower lei with music, hula, food, and sales of fantastic leis. May 1.

King Kamehameha Day—Parades, fairs, and other activities honor the king who united the islands. June.

Bon Odori Season—Buddhist festival that honors ancestors with music and dance. Late July/August.

Aloha Week—A celebration of Hawaii's culture, with music, dance, parades, crafts, food, and more. September/October.

For more information about the festivals and the exact dates, contact the visitors' information offices listed earlier.

Where to Stay

Choosing the right hotel and resort for you is not merely a matter of money. What's romantic and interesting for you may not be so for someone else. Some resorts are big and busy, with lots of organized activities. And some hotels and inns are small and low-key, preferring to leave their guests alone to enjoy the resort on their own. We feel that the resorts, hotels, and inns listed here are special places—each for its own reasons. Our price breakdown is as follows:

Expensive—$200 or more a night for a standard double room

Moderate—$100 to $200 a night for a standard double room

Inexpensive—Less than $100 a night for a standard double room.

At some resorts, meal plans are available that may save you money. The drawback is that the MAP (Modified American Plan) restricts your flexibility in trying restaurants elsewhere.

Our Choices on the East and North Shores:

Aston Kauai Resort—This recently renovated resort in Kapaa is a celebration of the floral beauty of the island. Colorful flowers and vines proliferate on the grounds and throughout the hotel, and the rooms' pastel colors and large picture windows bring this beauty inside. The 242 rooms are spacious and nicely furnished. The resort emphasizes Hawaii's history and culture, offers tours of nearby ruins, and provides Hawaiian entertainers on weekends. Facilities include a pool. Expensive. 3-5920 Kuhio Highway, Kapaa, HI 96747. 808/245–3931 or 800/922–7866.

Kay Barker's Bed & Breakfast—Ms. Barker is a lively octogenarian who has four modest guest rooms in her Kapaa home. Each room has a private bath. Inexpensive. P.O. Box 740, Kapaa, HI 96746. 808/822–3073.

Cliffs at Princeville—The location, on the cliffs overlooking the ocean at the northern shore, is dramatic, and the 200 units in the luxurious condominium complex are spacious and well equipped. Facilities include pool, tennis courts, and golf courses. Expensive. P.O. Box 1005, Hanalei, HI 96714. 808/826–6219.

Coco Palms Resort Hotel—The grande dame of Kauai resorts, this place has a history all its own. The queen of Kauai once owned the 45 acres on which it is located. Its thatched roof, Chapel in the Palms, was used by Rita Hayworth in the movie *Sadie Thompson.* And another king, Elvis, sang the "Hawaiian Wedding Song" here when he married Joan Blackman in the 1961 epic *Blue Hawaii.* The resort resembles a Hawaiian village, complete with thatched cottages, fish ponds, and lagoons. The rooms are spacious and lovely, furnished in Plantation Colonial style and decorated in white on pastel. There are 390 rooms, ranging from standard rooms to suites and cottages. The cottages are romantic retreats, with private tropical lanais and lava rock baths. Some even have jacuzzis. Facilities include a mile-long beach, three pools, nine tennis courts, and other sports. Moderate/expensive. P.O. Box 631, Lihue, HI 96766. 808/822–4921 or 800/542–2626.

Hanalei Bay Resort—Huge, fully furnished condo apartments, private gardens, and lots of activities make this 176-unit clifftop condo resort an exceptional find. The rooms offer great views of the bay and mountains. Facilities include two pools, tennis, and golf. Moderate. P.O. Box 220, Hanalei, HI 96714. 808/826–6522 or 800/367–7040.

Sheraton Mirage Princeville—Always beautiful, with some of the most stunning views in the islands, this resort has just undergone a massive facelift that will only make it more sensational. The views are outstanding: on one side is the summit called Bali Hai, on the other is the Hanalei Bay, and beyond that the rugged bluffs of the Na Pali Coast. The old hotel had 300 rooms; the renovated resort will have more rooms with larger accommodations. Facilities include a beach, pool, tennis, golf course, and sports facilities. Expensive. P.O. Box 3069, Princeville, HI 96722. 808/826–9644 or 800/334–8484.

Westin Kauai—Take a developer's image of Rome in its most decadent days, a few hundred million dollars, lots of water (and we mean lots of water) and you can transform the old Kauai Surf into an 849-room resort that blends the best and the worst of what money can buy. The Westin is an opulent wonderland: huge lagoons fed by spouting animal-shaped fountains lead to marble mazes that lead on to other excesses: a pool large enough to host a Super Bowl, with waterfalls and jacuzzis, surrounded by columned verandas; a series of restaurants connected by lagoons on which luxury yachts are used as shuttle buses; an 11-court tennis complex with a 1,000-seat stadium; a health spa that is so beautiful and so complete that words fail us; gardens; a wedding chapel on an island in the lagoon; exotic animals; golf courses; massive sculptures (they know what they like in art: big and heavy), and enough shops to stock a mall in your hometown. Oh, the rooms? Compared to the outside attractions, they are nice but small (too small to hold one of the sculptures). Facilities include everything, even a beach. Expensive. 3500 Rice St., Lihue, HI 96766. 808/245–5050 or 800/228–3000.

On the Southern Shore:

Gloria's Spouting Horn Bed and Breakfast Inn—This cute five-room B & B is on the ocean just west of the big resorts.

Inexpensive, breakfast included. 4464 Lawai Rd., Poipu, HI 96756. 808/742-6995.

Hyatt Regency Kauai—The newest of the big Hyatt resorts on the islands, this 605-room, $200 million playland will have a lagoon with its own islands, beaches, and endless activities. The rooms are spacious and nicely furnished, as always with Hyatt. Facilities include a golf course, four tennis courts, riding stables, beaches, two pools, and more. Expensive. 1571 Poipu Rd., Koloa, HI 96756. 808/742-1234 or 800/228-9000.

Kiahuna Plantation—The 333 rooms in this lovely oceanfront resort are in one- and two-bedroom cottages and low, garden-apartment–style buildings set in beautifully landscaped grounds. The rooms are comfortable and nicely decorated in tropical colors. Facilities include beach, pool, tennis, and golf. Expensive. R.R. 1, P.O. Box 73, Koloa, HI 96756. 808/742-6411 or 800/367-7052.

Kokee Lodge—For those tired of palm trees, tropical color schemes, rattan, and sand, this small mountain inn set in the pine trees on the north end of the Waimea Canyon may be a find. The lodge has 12 rustic cabins with fireplaces. Furnishings are simple. Inexpensive. P.O. Box 819, Waimea, HI 96796. 808/335-6061.

Koloa Landing Cottages—There are only four units in this cozy garden retreat near Poipu Beach—a pair of two-bedroom cottages and two studio apartments. Each is fully equipped, with kitchen and other amenities. Moderate. 2740-B Hoonanai Rd., Koloa, HI 96756. 808/742-1470.

Kuhio Shores—This 75-unit condominium offers spacious one- and two-bedroom apartments, all fully equipped, and all offer views of either the harbor or the Pacific. Expensive. R.R. 1, P.O. Box 70, Koloa, HI 96756. 800/367-8022 or 808/742-6120.

Stouffer Waiohai Beach Resort—This lovely beachfront resort offers superb rooms in a garden setting. The 460 rooms are spacious, with private patios or verandas overlooking center courtyards or, in the case of suites, the beach. Facilities include a beautiful open-air lobby, three pools, tennis, beach, and water sports. Expensive. 2249 Poipu Rd., Koloa, HI 96756. 808/742–9511 or 800/426–4122.

Sheraton Kauai Hotel—What struck us most about this oceanfront resort is that we think the best rooms (and by far the better rate) are not on the beach but across the way in the gardens. The 114-room Ocean Wing, just undergoing expansion and renovation, has nice rooms just steps away from the series of crescent-shaped white sand beaches. The 226-room Garden Wing, though, has larger and more attractive accommodations with views of the lovely gardens surrounding you. It's only a one-minute walk to the water. Facilities include tennis, water sports, and two pools. Expensive. R.R. 1, P.O. Box 303, Koloa, HI 96756. 808/742–1661 and 800/334–8484.

Victoria Place—This small (four rooms) B & B offers simple but nicely done rooms and is a short drive from Poipu Beach. Inexpensive, breakfast included. P.O. Box 930, Lawai, HI 96756. 808/332–9330.

For more listings of B & Bs, call Bed & Breakfast-Hawaii at 800/657–7832; Bed & Breakfast Honolulu (statewide listings) at 800/288–4666, ext. 351, B & B Kauai at 808/822–7771 and 800/367–8047, ext. 339, or Bed & Breakfast Pacific-Hawaii at 808/254–5030.

Where to Dine

The better restaurants on the islands are usually in the finest resorts. However, for those willing to venture outside their resort or hotel, some special dining rooms await. Always make reservations and always ask about the dress code.

The price categories for restaurants, for two persons for dinner, excluding wine, alcohol, tips, and taxes, are:

Expensive—More than $75.
Moderate—$25 to $75.
Inexpensive—Less than $25.

Our Choices on the East and North Shore:

Aloha Diner—It isn't a romantic dining room, but the saimin (noodles) and the fantastic chicken and seafood dishes make this casual Waipouli dining room a special place. Inexpensive. 971-F Kuhio Highway, Waipouli. 808/822–3851.

Bull Shed—Despite its tacky name, this Waipouli restaurant serves excellent steak, lamb, and seafood. There are two locations, the original at 796 Kuhio Highway in Kapaa (808/822–3791) and the new spot in the Menehune Shopping Village in Lihue (808/245–4551). Moderate.

Casa di Amici—The menu is classic Italian, from the antipasto to the desserts, at this famous north shore restaurant. Moderate. 2484 Keneke St., Kilauea. 808/828–1388.

Hanalei Dolphin—This cozy oceanfront north shore restaurant serves excellent local seafood, but don't miss the Hawaiian chicken. Moderate/expensive. Hanalei. 808/826–6113.

Hanamaulu Cafe—The setting is serene: a teahouse with koi ponds and lovely, tranquil gardens. The cuisine is Japanese, so stick to the seafood and open-grill steak or try the chef's nine-course special. Inexpensive. Highway 56, Hanamaulu. 808/245–2511.

Kapaa Fish and Chowder House—Seafood is the attraction here, served with a cajun accent. Try the seafood with pasta or the kiawe-broiled fish. Moderate. 4-1639 Kuhio Highway, Kapaa. 808/822–7488.

Kintaro—Classic Japanese cuisine in a restaurant that looks like it was designed in Tokyo (white rice paper screens, blonde wood furnishings). Moderate. 4-370 Kuhio Highway, Wailua. 808/822–3341.

Pacific Cafe—Creative seafood, blending the accents of both Asia and Europe, make this Kapaa restaurant an outstanding attraction. Expensive. Kauai Village on the Kuhio Highway in Kapaa. 808/822–0013.

Westin Kauai—This megaresort has a number of excellent restaurants. Try The Masters, a very formal and very elegant dining room with a French menu, or the more casual Inn at the Cliffs, which offers superb seafood and pasta dishes. Both are expensive. Call 808/245–5050 for reservations at either restaurant.

Our Choices on the Southern Shore:

Gaylord's—You dine in the backyard of the Wilcox Mansion at Kilohana, the restored sugar plantation just west of Lihue. The lamb, veal, and chicken dishes are superb, but the best meal here is the Sunday brunch. Expensive. On Highway 50 west of Lihue. 808/245-9593.

Kiahuna Plantation—The best dining room at this resort is the Plantation Gardens Restaurant, which serves excellent steaks and seafood on a lovely veranda. Moderate. Poipu. 808/742-1695.

Koloa Fish and Chowder House—Seafood is the attraction, served with a cajun accent, at this southern branch of the Kapaa restaurant. Try the seafood with pasta or the kiawe-broiled fish. Moderate. 5402 Koloa Rd., Koloa. 808/742-7377.

Sheraton Kauai Hotel—Naniwa is the outstanding restaurant at this resort. Decorated like a Japanese country inn and located next to a koi lagoon, this elegant dining spot serves excellent and authentic Japanese dishes. Expensive. 808/742-1661.

Stouffer Waiohai—This fine resort has several fine restaurants, but our favorite is the Tamarind, which has a slick, modern decor and a romantic atmosphere. The Tamarind serves a mix of continental and Pacific Rim cuisine. The charred sashimi, duck, and seafood dishes were excellent. Expensive. 2249 Poipu Rd., Poipu. 808/742-9511.

Tashio—Sushi and other traditional Japanese dishes have made this Koloa restaurant popular with locals and tourists alike. Moderate. Koloa. 808/742-1838.

Luaus and Other Nightlife

The best luaus are at the big resorts. On the eastern shore, the Aston Kauai resort has a Polynesian Show on Monday, Wednesday, Fridays, and Saturdays (808/245-3931); the Coco Palms has its Polynesian Show Tuesdays through Saturdays (808/822-4921); and Smith's Tropical Paradise has its luaus weeknights

(808/822–4654). On the south shore, the Stouffer Waiohai Beach Resort has an excellent, well-staged luau on Monday nights (808/742–9511). The best on the island may be at the Tahiti Nui, a small Hanalei spot offering more fun than these professional shows. It's too bad it's so far from the big resorts. Call 808/826–6277. Luau and show prices start at about $30 per person.

For other nightlife, try the big resorts—the Westin and the new Hyatt. They have live bands in their nightclubs.

The magnificent Lodge at Koele, the first major resort on Lanai.
(Photo courtesy of Barbara Radin-Fox)

CHAPTER 3

Lanai: The Undiscovered Island

I waena oka Pakipika, aia 'o Hawai'i.
I waena 'o Hawai'i, aia 'o Lana'i.
Aia ika mole 'o Lana'i, 'o Koele.
E ho'okipa, ai i Ko'ele.

In the middle of the Pacific, there is Hawaii.
In the center of Hawaii, there is Lanai.
In the heart of Lanai, is Koele.
Welcome to Koele.

*W*ithin sight of the crowded shores of Maui and the bluffs of Molokai, and only minutes by air from Oahu, Hawaii, and Kauai, is the often-overlooked Lanai. Smaller than its five sister islands, Lanai has often been bypassed by visitors who think that this mostly agricultural island holds few charms. How wrong they are. And now that RockResorts and the island's owner, Castle & Cooke, have joined together to create two exciting, luxurious resorts on the island, there is even more reason for visiting Lanai. The island's 2,300 residents used to cherish their relative seclusion; now they wonder whether tourists will change Lanai.

For years the gourd-shaped, 140-square-mile island was ignored. In ancient times, a curse was said to be put on the land and that any residents would be haunted by evil spirits. The curse, real or not, was voided when Kaululaau, the son of a Maui king, was exiled to the island and proceeded to prove that either the demons did not exist or that he was more powerful than any spirit. For this, Kaululaau became a hero and attracted residents to his island.

These early years of habitation were rough. Battles between the island residents and the forces of Kamehameha took a heavy toll, and in the final conflict all but one of the islanders were slain. The land, too, made life difficult. Lanai's east side is wet, but its rugged mountains and impassable ravines are inhospitable, while the central plateau and the adjacent valleys are dry.

Captain James Cook, the explorer who discovered the islands in 1778, described Lanai as dry, barren, and thoroughly unattractive for colonization.

The Mormons and other missionaries came and formed huge ranches. Their efforts failed when overgrazing turned Lanai into a ruin and a land dispute divided the mission. By 1910, all the separate parcels of land were bought up and joined together as the Koele Ranch.

By then, the island was a mess, with few trees, almost no vegetation, and little hope that it would ever improve. But it did change, mainly because of the keen observation of a New Zealander who managed the Koele Ranch and because James Dole had the crazy idea he could grow pineapples on the island.

The New Zealander who helped save Lanai was George Munro, a naturalist who erected fences to pen the livestock, built windbreaks, and worked to protect the few groves of trees left. All of this helped, but none so much as the discovery he made one night when the clouds were rolling over the mountainside near his house.

Munro heard drops of water hitting his house. When he came out to look, he noticed that the branches of the tall Norfolk pine tree next to the house were acting as filters, removing the moisture from the clouds always passing over the higher land on the island.

Munro ordered his ranch hands to begin planting the trees. As more were planted, Lanai became wetter and greener. In time, the eastern shore became a thick forest, offering refuge to numerous other trees and plants, some rarely seen on the more developed islands.

The second major change came in 1921, when James Dole bought all but 2 percent of the island and began planting pineapples in the flat Palawi Basin. Dole's plantation was a success, until the difficult days of the Depression, when he was forced to sell out to Castle & Cooke.

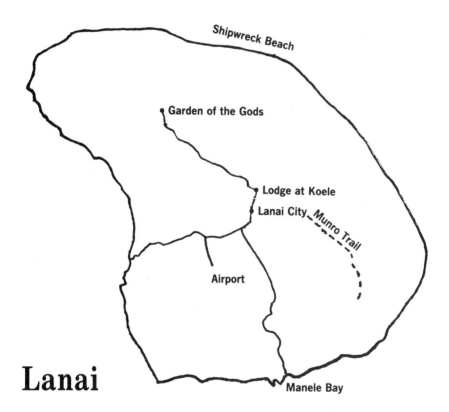

Shipwreck Beach

Garden of the Gods

Lodge at Koele

Lanai City Munro Trail

Airport

Lanai

Manele Bay

The pineapples were both a bounty and a curse for the island's residents. It gave them work, but the plantation-style life and the monopoly of land ownership kept development and tourism far from the island.

That was unfortunate, not only for the island residents but for visitors, for Lanai is a beautiful island, made up of dramatic green mountains and ravines, sweeping coastal plains unmarked by condos or other development, and groves of the majestic Norfolk pine. Visitors may enjoy two magnificent resorts, nature trails, lovely beaches devoid of any sign of life, ancient rock carvings and ruins of royal retreats, a wide variety of animal life, and some of the most unusual and interesting landscape west of the desert of the Southwest on the mainland.

Describing Lanai requires a lot of "onlys" and "nos." There are only three roads and only one city on the island. There are only 2,300 residents on the island, and almost all of them live in that single town, Lanai City. For them, life is fairly uncomplicated. There are no movie houses, no arcades, no athletic fields on the island. The residents' pleasures revolve around family (many of the residents are related), work, fishing, and hunting.

Their life seems so simple, so basic, that it isn't until the predawn hours that the pineapple fields exact their own price. For at 4:30 every morning, long before any tourist would rise, the scream of a whistle sounds through the quiet streets of tiny Lanai City, passing on the command: There is work to be done in the fields. Report in 90 minutes.

Touring the Island

There is only one place to start and that is Lanai City, the only community on the island and the place where all the island roads—all three of them—meet.

Lanai City is a company town located almost in the center of the 17-by-12-mile, gourd-shaped island. The town is 1,600 feet above sea level, and is a sharp contrast to the slick resort strips on Oahu or Maui. The island residents, most of whom work either for Dole or in the new resorts, live in modest, colorful frame bungalows on the small streets that form a grid pattern surrounding the city park, a pleasant green area surrounded by business and civic buildings and shaded by tall Norfolk pines.

The streets are usually quiet in this village. You will find some activity at the various civic buildings or the churches. Shopping is limited, but basic wares can be found at Richard's, at 434 Eighth Avenue, and the Pine Isle Market, 356 Eighth Avenue.

The few dining alternatives outside the resorts are also found in Lanai City. Dahang's Pastry Shop at 409 Seventh Avenue serves delicious pastries, and the building labeled S.T. Properties, Inc., at 419 Seventh Avenue is locally famous for its burgers and sandwiches. The Hotel Lanai, a simple frame building on a tree-shaded lot on Highway 44 on the east side of town, offers ten plain rooms and a dining room serving modest meals. This may change, for RockResorts is taking over management of the inn.

There are some curious sights in town: the blue outhouselike structures next to the police station are where lawbreakers (usually drunks) are held, the Ito Gardens are a short walk from the Hotel Lanai, and the Old Plantation Manager's House is located in the woods above town. The house has been restored and is now used as a public meeting hall.

That's all of the attractions in town. The real beauty of Lanai, the rarely seen forests, valleys, beaches, and ruins are outside the village, often reached by dirt roads that aren't marked and don't always appear on the maps.

There is no public transportation on the island, so getting around requires either joining the few guided tours or renting your own car, preferably a four-wheel drive vehicle. If you do drive yourself, be patient; the roads are poorly marked, and most aren't paved. Don't drive into the mountains without a four-wheel-drive car.

However you go, a tour should start by heading west on Highway 440, which is the main road to the airport, the pineapple fields, and Kaumalapau Harbor.

The land is comprised of red earth here, and the pineapple

plants grow in orderly rows. It takes 18 months to 2 years for a mature pineapple to grow on a stalk on the cactuslike plant with the sharp, sword-shaped leaves. The first fruit weighs about four or five pounds. The second-crop pineapples are smaller, and usually grow two per plant. By the third crop, the pineapples are too small to harvest, and are used for seeding fields.

It's against the law to pick the pineapples, but it's done with some frequency. Despite the millions of pineapples around us, most of the pineapple juice we were served on the island was canned because almost all of the fruit is shipped away.

Highway 440 continues west through the fields and down to the harbor, where the picked fruit is shipped out. From this point, look north and south of the harbor to view the dramatic coastline.

Retrace your drive and take Highway 440 south until it makes a sharp right turn. Continue on it for a mile until you come to a dirt road leading off to the left and into the pineapple fields. The road ends at a dry ditch. Cross the ditch on foot and climb up the steep hill to the giant black boulders. On these rocks are the Luahiwa Petroglyphs: carvings of a man, a turtle, a canoe, and other animals.

The carvings are believed to have been made in the early nineteenth century, but their significance is unknown. One local expert suggested that the hillside location overlooking the Palawi Basin is on a line with the ruins of Kaunolu, King Kamehameha's fishing village on Lanai.

Return to Highway 440 and drive south until the highway makes a sharp left where Kaupili Road comes in. Take this new road through the fields until you come to the fourth dirt road, unmarked of course, and drive down to the ocean and the stone platforms and other ruins of Kaunolu. There are more than 80 houses and 35 shelters in this excavated ruin.

Return back to Highway 440 and turn south again to Manele Bay, a beautiful shore spot guarded by lava cliffs hundreds of feet high. The bay on the left is Hulopoe Beach, a magnificent crescent of white sand where the superluxurious Manele Bay Hotel is located. The beach here is the best on the island, at least the best beach that can be accessed with ease. Another fine beach is at Club Lanai, an eight-acre beach club on the island's eastern shore. You can reach the club by sailing from Maui. The cruise includes breakfast on board, lunch, bus tours of island sights, and water sports. Call 808/871–1144.

Return on Highway 440 to Lanai City and drive north on Lanai Avenue (Highway 44) out of town for two miles until you come to a gravel road on the right. Turn onto it, for this is the beginning of the eight-mile-long Munro Trail, a difficult drive in good weather and impossible in bad. The trail is also popular with hikers and horseback riders, for it climbs almost 2,000 feet through a dense and lovely rain forest to the 3,370-foot-high Lanaihale, the island's summit.

Along the way are trails leading to overlooks. One takes you to a perch overlooking Hauola Gulch, where all but one of the island's residents were slain during a battle in 1778. The notches in the spine of the green ridge were cut by the residents, who threw rocks down at the invaders approaching them through the gorgeous Maunalei Gulch.

From this point you can see Molokai, Maui, and the lovely coastal plain of Lanai. It's an unusual sight in these islands, which are always busy with construction of newer, grander resorts. The plain is entirely unspoiled: no condos, no highways—nothing.

The Munro Trail continues south to join with a dirt road that leads west to Highway 440 south. Or you can return back to Highway 44 and take it north, down to the coast. This route leads down to unpaved roads that parallel the shore. To the left, or north, is Shipwreck Beach, an area popular with the Filipino residents of Lanai. They have built flimsy and colorful shacks there—locals call it the Filipino Federation—where they spend weekends fishing and playing. The beach gets its name from the *Liberty* ship now rusting away just offshore. It was driven onto the reef during World War II by the strong winds that blow toward the shore from the channel between Molokai and Maui.

East of Highway 44 along the beach are the ruins of several

old fishing villages. They are interesting, but are not worth the drive unless you are a real history buff.

As you drive along you may notice the small pyramids of stacked stones that are just off the road. These are road markers, placed by residents decades ago when the trek down to the shore was treacherous and often made in horse-drawn wagons. The rocks marked the safe way down.

The final attraction on the island is the Garden of the Gods, which sounds better than it is. A dirt road leading off Highway 44 north of Lanai City takes you to the Garden, a wind carved gorge of strange shapes and colors. It is beautiful, and the colors evoke images of the desert of the Southwest.

For More Information

There are no visitor bureaus on the island. Contact the Maui Visitors' Bureau at 380 Dairy Rd., Kahului, HI 96732, 808/871–8691. The bureau has information about Lanai.

Festivals

Lanai, like all the islands, celebrates the following festivals, but the population is so small that the festivities will probably go unnoticed.

Cherry Blossom Festival—A celebration of Japanese culture and heritage, with music, dance, and food featured. Late February/early March.

Buddha Day—A pageant of flowers with parades and other activities. April.

Lei Day—Celebration of the flower lei with music, hula, food, and sales of fantastic leis. May 1.

King Kamehameha Day—Parades, fairs, and other activities honor the king who united the islands. June.

Bon Odori Season—Buddhist festival that honors ancestors with music and dance. Late July/August.

Aloha Week—A celebration of Hawaii's culture, with music, dance, parades, crafts, food, and more. September/October.

HAWAII'S SYSTEM OF TABOO

For more than four centuries, life in Hawaii was governed by a series of strictly enforced laws and religious decrees that controlled every aspect of the islanders' lives. This system was called the *kapu,* or taboo system, and the rules prohibited commoners from touching a chief or walking in his footsteps, prevented women from eating with men, and regulated hunting and fishing seasons. The islanders feared that the gods would punish kapu violators with a tidal wave, volcanic eruption, or other natural disaster.

Playing a major role in the kapu system were the heiaus, or temples. Here the *kahunas* (priests) and *aliis* (chiefs) ruled and dictated what sacrifices should be made to appease the gods. Occasionally, the sacrifices were human.

The heiaus also served as a place of sanctuary where the kapu violators could flee and be purified by the priests. The massive stone platforms of some heiaus can be viewed today. The Puuhonua O Honaunau on Hawaii, the Iliiliopae on Molokai, and the Kaneaki Heiau on Oahu are the most interesting.

The kapu system ended in October 1819 when King Kamehameha's son, Liholiho, ascended to the throne after the death of his father. Liholiho, now known as King Kamehameha II, abolished the system at the urging of Queen Kaahumanu, the "favorite" wife of the king's father, Kamehameha I, and Queen Keopuolani, his mother. These two strong-willed women had long objected to the restrictions placed on the activities and power of women, particularly those who were chiefs in their own right.

The two queens and the young king marked the end of the kapu system with a feast at which a number of men and women ate together. When the gods did not retaliate, King Kamehameha II abolished the kapu system.

For more information about the festivals and the exact dates, contact the Maui Visitors' Bureau listed earlier.

Where to Stay

There isn't much to choose from on this island. The Lodge at Koele opened in May 1990 and is one of the finest mountain resorts we have ever visited. The 102-room lodge is styled after a country estate, and has a main building faced with a porch that stretches almost its entire width and encompasses the two galleries that lead to the wings of guest rooms. A small foyer lined with antiques (the odd, cartlike device on the left is a saddle of an elephant) leads into a 35-foot-high Great Hall flanked by massive stone fireplaces and opens to a wall of glass, through which you can see the croquet lawns, beautiful pool, orchid greenhouse, gardens of exotic flowers and waterfalls, and a large lake next to a gazebo and giant banyan trees.

The view is stunning, almost as striking as the marvelous paintings, crafts, and quilts that decorate the large room, most of which were created by 35 island artists. The feeling of being in a museum is completed by the large collection of paintings, antiques, sculptures, artifacts, and other items from Europe, Asia, and other Pacific islands. The effect is spectacular, creating a setting that rivals the hunting lodge of an industrial baron.

The art continues in the 12 plantation suites, located off the balcony overlooking the Great Hall, and the 90 rooms in the two wings. The rooms are furnished with more pieces of art and crafts: headboards are painted, the window seats have quilted pillows, and the walls are decorated with paintings of native flora. Each suite and room has a porch or balcony overlooking the lawns.

Facilities include a pool, croquet courts, tennis, 18-hole Greg Norman golf course, an excellent and challenging 18-hole miniature golf course with real grass greens, a music room, organized craft and cultural activities, and endless beauty. Other recreational activities include jeep rides, horseback riding, bikes, tennis, and beach trips.

Room rates are expensive, starting at more than $200 per night. A meal plan is available.

The companion resort, the Manele Bay Hotel has 250 luxury suites and rooms on Hulopoe Bay and its crescent beach. The resort, which is to open in the second half of 1991, will have furnishings and activities that we are certain will match those at the Lodge at Koele. Room rates will be as expensive as, if not more than, those at the Lodge. For more information about either resort, call 800/223–7637.

Where to Dine

Your choices are very limited, but are you in luck! Rush over to the main dining room at the Lodge at Koele, where some of the most marvelous dishes we have ever tasted await. Try the axis deer, the lamb chops, or the mahimahi. In fact, take out a second mortgage, stay a week, and try it all. And don't miss the breakfasts. They are the kind of feasts that make you wobble off to find a quiet place in the sun in which to snooze and recover. It's all expensive, of course, but in this case it's worth every penny. Call 808/548–3768.

When the Manele Bay Hotel opens, the Lodge will have some competition. We expect the high quality of the Lodge's dining room will be matched by the newer resort.

Luaus and Other Nightlife

There are no luaus, at least not at the time of this writing, and the little nightlife there is, happens only at the resorts, which offer Hawaiian folk entertainment.

The strange and forbidding landscape inside the crater of Haleakala. *(Hawaii Visitors Bureau; photo by Anthony Anjo)*

CHAPTER 4

Maui: The Cosmopolitan Island

*M*aui has it all: beautiful beaches, elegant resorts and villa communities, gorgeous golf courses, magnificent mountains and valleys filled with extraordinary foliage and landscape.

Hawaiians call Maui "No Ka Oi," which simply means "the best." Maui has earned the praise. A generation ago, the 729-square-mile island was more popular with sugarcane producers than with sunseekers. Since then, the island has changed its image from that of an agricultural island to one that is more sophisticated than its sister islands.

The change came when the island's leaders decided to lure more visitors, particularly those in the upper tax brackets. Large luxury resorts were built, and older hotels were renovated and upgraded. Superb condominium and villa communities sprang up, followed by golf courses and tennis complexes, and in turn by galleries and boutiques aimed at the upscale shopper.

By the start of the 1990s, Maui had been transformed from an agricultural backwater to an international hot spot, one where millionaires were more common than in any other spot in the United States.

With all this, one might get the impression that Maui had little to offer outside these playgrounds for the upscale traveler. That would be very wrong, for Maui is filled with natural wonders and interesting towns.

The island is actually formed by the marriage of what once were two separate islands, each created by their own volcano. Erosion and further eruptions slowly closed the channel between the islands, creating a low plain linking the two on a northwest-to-southeast axis. The plain looks like a valley between the two volcanos, hence Maui's other nickname, the Valley Isle.

West Maui is the region northwest of the valley. It's dominated by the 5,788-foot Puu Kukui, an extinct volcano whose steep slopes and rugged ravines are often shrouded in mist from the 400 inches of rain that fall there each year. This end of the island is home to the old royal retreat and whaling village of Lahaina, the Kaanapali resorts, and lush rain forests.

Across the valley is eastern Maui, the larger part of the island. It's dominated by the 10,023-foot Haleakala, a dormant volcano whose summit is often hidden in clouds. Haleakala is an alien land, one whose crater resembles the landscape of the moon. The summit is popular with the adventurous who rise early and drive to the summit to see the spectacular sunrise.

The eastern slopes of Haleakala and the small town of Hana are covered by a thick, green jungle fed by the rains that fall on this side of the island.

The western shore of this part of Maui is drier, but no less attractive. Offshore is the partially sunken crater of Molokini, a popular place with divers and snorkelers. In the Wailea area are the finer resorts, the luxury condos and villas, numerous beaches, and the large golf and tennis facilities. This is the playground of the wealthy.

Getting around Maui is fairly easy, though the road from Hana around the south side of Haleakala requires a four-wheel-drive vehicle and lots of time and patience. Maui does have traffic jams, particularly around Lahaina on the northwest coast and in the main town of Kahului. By mainland and Oahu standards, these traffic bottlenecks aren't much, but should be considered if you are traveling to a dinner appointment.

To help you tour Maui, we have broken the island into these four tours: Kahului and West Maui, The Road to Hana and Beyond, Haleakala and the Upcountry, and Wailea and Kihei.

Kahului and West Maui

Kahului is the commercial center of the island, the town visitors first encounter after leaving the airport. It was built in the 1950s as a planned community for employees of Alexander & Baldwin, a major producer of sugarcane in the islands. Many island

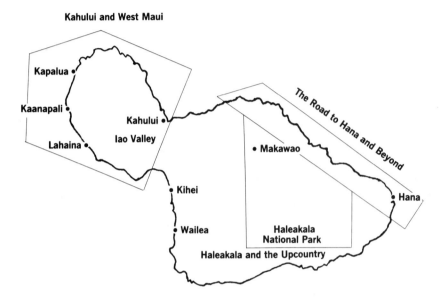

Kahului and West Maui

Kapalua •

Kaanapali •

Lahaina •

Kahului •
Iao Valley

• Kihei

• Wailea

The Road to Hana and Beyond

• Makawao

• Hana

Haleakala
National Park

Haleakala and the Upcountry

Maui

residents live here, surrounded by shopping centers, fast-food restaurants, hardware stores, and other outlets.

Beyond the commercial centers, there are a few attractions in and just outside of town. In Puunene, a small town southeast of Kahului, is the Alexander & Baldwin Sugar Museum. The museum, at 3957 Hansen Road, is located in the restored house of a sugar plantation manager, and displays artifacts and exhibits tracing the history of sugarcane production on Maui.

The other attractions are west of town. From town take Highway 340 along the shore, turn on Kuhio Place and follow the signs to the Halekii, a huge (150-foot-by-300-foot) temple used during the rule of Kahekili during the late 1700s. About 100 yards away is the Pihana Heiau State Monument, a temple used for sacrifices around the time of the American Revolution.

More attractions lie west of town, on Highway 32 (Kaahumanu Avenue). Drive west on this road and turn north on Kanaloa Avenue for the Maui Zoological and Botanical Gardens. The free gardens are open daily, but the emphasis here is on the animals rather than the exotic plants.

Continue west on Kaahumanu Avenue to Wailuku and that town's historic district. The old, wooden homes and buildings along High Street between Aupini and Main streets are interesting and colorful survivors of an age when life was less frantic. The most interesting buildings include the Kaahumanu Church, at High and Main streets, a classic New England–style structure built in 1876 on the site where Queen Kaahumanu was said to have worshipped. Services in the Hawaiian language are held every Sunday at 9 AM.

The Iao Theater at 68 North Market Street, reflects the art deco style popular in 1927 when it was built. It is open only during performances by a local theater group. The Hale Hoikeike, at 2375A Main Street, was built between 1838–1850 as the home of Edward and Caroline Bailey, two missionaries who came to Maui to run a girls' school. The house, made of stone and mortar, is now run by the Maui Historical Society and serves as a museum of Hawaiian artifacts. It is open daily from 10:00 AM to 4:30 PM.

Main Street leads out of Wailuku to the mountains and turns into the Iao Valley Road. The road passes by the Kepaniwai Heritage Gardens, a park with gardens and pavilions celebrating the islands' diverse cultures. The park is also the site of a bloody battle in which Kamehameha I defeated the Maui king in 1790.

A mile farther west is the Iao Valley Park, which was called the Yosemite of the Pacific by none other than Mark Twain. The valley is dominated by a huge green tower, the 2,250-foot high Iao Needle. The valley is a lush garden, hidden often by mists, colored by rainbows, and decorated by flowers and plants of every color. Take the paths leading from the parking area into the valley for even more striking views of the Needle and the surrounding countryside.

Retrace your steps and drive east again to Highway 30 and turn south for Lahaina and the Kaanapali resorts. The landscape quickly changes from the commercial and residential streets of Kahului and Wailuku to fields of sugarcane and more dramatic hills and ravines. After the road meets the coast and bears west to Lahaina, the coastal scenery is even more dramatic. Cliffs of deep red earth and stone combine with the bright aquamarine sea to form a colorful setting. Along the way to Lahaina are several seashore parks. The Launiupoko State Park and the Puamana Beach Park between Olowalu and Lahaina are popular with islanders and visitors for fishing, surfing, and swimming.

Lahaina is the most historic town on Maui. King Kamehameha lived here after conquering the island. The town also attracted the island's first missionaries and thousands of whalers who came to hunt the humpback whales wintering offshore. Modern-day Lahaina is a mixture of past and present. Narrow streets lined with huge trees and quaint cottages are flanked by a busy shopping and residential area that sprouted up along Highway 30.

Turn off Highway 30 and drive toward the sea until you come to Front Street. Front Street, the short Wharf Street facing the harbor, and the cross streets between the two make up the National Historic Landmark section of the city. These streets are home to many shops and restaurants and a few historic buildings. At all times, day or night, the area is a small circus, with crowds of sightseers, shoppers, and fun-seekers.

The shopping begins at the south end, at 505 Front Street, where you will find a small maze of shops selling leather and jewelry. A short walk north, beyond the small residential area, at Wharf and Hotel street is a magnificent banyan tree that was planted in 1873. Next to it, facing Wharf Street, is the Court House, which was built in 1859 and renovated in 1925. The Court House now holds art galleries. The Old Jail Gallery, located in what once was the prison in the basement, sells some fine works by Maui artists.

Other art galleries can be found nearby on Front Street. At 697, the Front Street Gallery sells paintings and prints and at 758 Front Street, the Grycner sells a wide variety of works by artists from the island and the mainland.

Continue walking down to the water until you come to the harbor and the Carthaginian II, a 93-foot copy of the type of vessel that brought immigrants to the islands in the nineteenth century. The ship holds a whaling museum. It's open daily from 10:00 AM to 4:00 PM.

On Papelekane Street, a block from the ship in front of the old Pioneer Inn, are the ruins of the Brick Palace, a western-style structure built by King Kamehameha I. He lived in it only for a year.

At 696 Front Street is the Baldwin Home Museum, the New England–style home of Dwight Baldwin, a doctor and missionary who came to Maui in the early 1800s. The house was built in 1834 of coral and island wood. It has been restored and furnished to display the lifestyle of the Baldwins. The museum is open daily from 9:30 AM to 4:30 PM.

Maui's oldest building, the Master's Reading Room, is located next to the Baldwin house. The building, a reading area for master sailors, was built by sailors and missionaries in 1834.

A short walk north on Front Street brings you to the Lahaina Scrimshaw Factory, where the ivory art (mostly on fossilized walrus tusks) is carved, engraved, and sold.

Continue north on Front Street to the Wharf Shopping Center, where you can also see the Spring House, a structure erected by missionaries to shield a freshwater spring. Farther north, at 858 Front Street, is the Wo Hing Society, originally a temple but now a museum displaying Chinese relics. Films of Hawaii made by Thomas Edison in 1898 are shown in the theater. The museum is open Monday–Saturday from 9:00 AM to 4:30 PM, and Sunday from noon to 4:30 PM.

Your final stop is the historic Seamen's Hospital at 1024 Front Street. It was built for whalers in the 1840s and now is used by a printshop that sells antique maps and charts.

Return to Highway 30 and turn north toward Kaanapali. As you leave Lahaina you pass by a number of small malls featuring T-shirt shops, souvenir outlets, and clothing stores.

If you are fascinated by trains, you would probably like the Sugarcane Train, a turn-of-the-century steam engine that takes passengers into the cane fields and other scenic sights along the coast. Six one-hour roundtrips are made daily from the depot at Highway 30 and Lahainaluna Road; call 808/661–0089.

From the station, Highway 30 leads into the Kaanapali resort strip where you find the fine Kaanapali Beach and the Hyatt, Westin, and other large hotels. Whalers Village Shopping Center, located just north of the Westin Maui at 2435 Kaanapali Parkway, offers an outstanding collection of shops and restaurants. The Ka Honu Gift Gallery, Silk Kaanapali, Painted Lady, and Liberty House sell splendid gifts, crafts, and clothing. While here, stop in at the interesting Whalers Village Museum and its exhibits that explore the history of whaling in the island.

The Kaanapali Beach in front of the resorts is a lovely stretch of sand, but not a quiet shore for resting. Surfers, sailors, and water sports of all kinds make this beach the busiest on the island.

Beyond Kaanapali, Highway 30 continues to Kapalua, a town that is becoming popular with luxury condo developers, before passing several fine beaches on its way to the quieter villages of Honokohau and Kahakuloa.

The rugged and beautiful northwest shore has many fine

beaches. The best are at Napali Beach, Onela Beach, D. T. Fleming Park, Makuleia Bay (Slaughterhouse Beach), and Honolua Bay. The last two beaches are popular with snorkelers, for the waters are filled with so much marine life that they have been designated marine conservation districts.

Beyond the beaches and villages, Highway 30 ends, giving way to Highway 34, which in bad weather can become impassable. If you have the time, this drive is worth the effort. Kahakuloa is a small fishing village seemingly unchanged by time, and the wild coastline and hills here are perfect for snorkeling or hiking.

It is here, at the far northern end of Maui, that you can see how the island was before this beautiful island was discovered and became an "in" spot. The true beauty and wealth of Maui isn't at the resorts of marble and glass; it is here, at road's end, where the lush jungle meets the sea.

The Road to Hana and Beyond

From Kahului, Highway 36 curves along the coast, passing by some wonderful beaches and through several colorful and quaint towns before twisting through more than 600 sharp turns and crossing some 65 bridges and entering Hana, a region of lush jungle and dramatic coastline that earns its nickname "heavenly Hana."

The 55-mile drive to Hana is lined with some wonderful sights. The first you will come across is the H. A. Baldwin Park, a beachfront area popular with surfers and picnickers, followed quickly by the small crossroads village of Lower Paia. It's a quaint place, one that recalls street scenes from a western movie or television series. The storefronts are faded, but retain some color and dignity. Despite their sad appearance, these buildings house some interesting shops. The Maui Crafts Guild at 43 Hana Highway (Highway 36) displays and sells the excellent creations of island artists, while Rhonda's Bears Forever at 76 Hana Highway sells beautiful Hawaiian quilts.

THE SEASON OF WHALES

Winter is the prime tourist season in Hawaii, not only for two-legged visitors from the mainland but also for some 45-foot-long guests from the Bering Sea.

Each winter, humpback whales return to the warm waters around Hawaii to breed and bear their young. About 600 or so humpback whales make the journey, usually arriving in December and returning north by late April.

In the early 1800s, the winter migration of the humpbacks was an event attracting hundreds of whalers to the islands. Many used the port at Lahaina on Maui. More than 14,000 of the whales were believed to be in existence then, but the hunters, environmental pollution, and other man-made dangers have reduced their population to less than 1,000. The whales are protected by international treaty, but diplomacy hasn't prevented the herds from continuing to slowly shrink.

The whales are a fantastic sight. We urge you to take a whale-watching cruise, for when seen up close the whales are among the most majestic and moving sights in nature. A number of cruise ships sail from Maui and other islands to take a closer look at these mammoth mammals. Call Pacific Whale Foundation (808/879–8811 and 800/WHALE–1–1). On Maui, call Ocean Activities Center (808/879–4484), Alihilani Charters (808/871–1156), Seabird Excursions (808/661–3643), Leilani Cruises (808/661–8397), and Trilogy Excursions (808/661–4743). The cruises cost from $35 per person and up.

East of Paia, Highway 36 bypasses Hookpia Beach Park, a shore popular with surfers, before entering the rugged coastal area. The next sight is Twin Falls, a beautiful swimming area with two waterfalls. Park near the first bridge you encounter and look for the marked trail to the falls. A quarter mile farther on the trail is another, larger swimming hole, but with only one waterfall.

The scenery in this area is stunning. The road clings to a cliff covered with ferns, breadfruit, koa, and other plants and trees common to Hawaii's rain forests. Waterfalls, rushing streams, and small parks offer numerous temptations for you to stop and linger. The small villages you pass through—Pauwela, Huelo, and Kailua—are interesting, but not remarkable enough for anything more than a brief stop.

Past Kailua is Kaumahina State Park, a pleasant clifftop area with striking views of the coastline. A mile farther is Honomau Valley, a gorge with 3,000-foot walls and a 1,000-foot waterfall that is almost inaccessible. Don't try to hike into it.

Beyond the valley is the village of Keanae and its Arboretum, a small garden with numerous exotic flowers and plants. Just beyond these gardens is the Keanae Overlook, roughly the half-way point on the drive to Hana. The overlook offers grand views of the wonders of land and sea.

More overlooks await you east of Keanae. Three miles past the town is the Wailua Overlook and, down by the coast, Wailua, a village inhabited by taro farmers.

The scenery keeps getting better. Less than a half-mile east of Wailua is Waikane Falls, a dramatic waterfall well worth stopping to observe, and photograph.

The next town on the Hana Highway is Nahiku, a dying plantation village whose population is now less than 100. Beyond this village is Waianapanapa State Park, an oceanfront park that is popular with swimmers. Hiking trails lead throughout the park, including to two lava caverns. Legends say a Hawaiian princess was slain by a jealous husband in the Waianapanapa Cavern. (The state rents cabins at the park for a very small fee; call 808/ 248–8061.)

Three miles farther on the Hana Highway are the Helani Gardens, 60 acres of unusual flowers and trees. The gardens are open from 10:00 AM to 4:00 PM daily.

The next stop is Hana. After such a long drive, the town itself may be a disappointment. Hana is famous for the luxurious Hotel Hana-Maui, one of the top resorts in the state, and the

Hale Waiwai O'Hana (House of Treasures of Hana). The Hale holds an interesting collection of photographs, quilts, crafts, shells, and other artifacts from this side of Maui. It's open from 11:00 AM to 4:00 PM daily except Sunday. One other famed landmark, the eclectic Hasegawa's Store, unfortunately burned down in the summer of 1990.

Kaihalulu Beach, a short walk from the Hana Community Center on Hauoli Road in town, is a red-sand beach that once was popular with nudists because of its isolation. That time has gone now, and families now crowd the shores of this lovely strand of beach.

Beyond Hana, the highway changes its name to the Piilani Highway and turns into an ill-maintained road filled with potholes. Now may be the time to turn around. If you continue, drive ten miles past Hana to Oheo Gulch, another swimming hole, and just a mile farther to the Hoomau Congregation Church, on whose grounds aviator Charles Lindbergh is buried.

Haleakala and the Upcountry

Mt. Haleakala is more than just a dormant volcano. Its eastern slopes are the watershed that feeds the lush rain forests of the Hana coast. Its western slopes are the farming and ranching centers of the island. And its summit—10,238 feet above the sea—is another world from that found down on the beaches or in the lush jungle.

On top of the mountain is a barren, eerie landscape of craters and plants not seen anywhere else. Even the weather is different, often 30 degrees cooler than the temperatures down at the resorts. Strong winds, rain, and even occasional snowstorms in the winter are common, and care must be taken before you go up to the summit. Clouds usually move in by noon, obscuring the view and making driving conditions more hazardous. So leave early and call 808/572-7749 for the weather conditions before you go.

From Kahului, drive southeast on Highway 37 (Haleakala

Highway) until the road splits into Highway 37 and Highway 377. Take Highway 377 and drive six miles to Haleakala Crater Road (Highway 378) and turn left on this route. This is a difficult road, filled with hairpin turns as it ascends the slopes of Mt. Haleakala. The Haleakala National Park Headquarters at the entrance and the Visitors' Center inside the park have exhibits, maps, and other information about the 28,665-acre park.

This park is a place of myths and wonder. According to legend, it was on the summit that the demigod Maui captured the sun and held it prisoner until the sun promised to move across the sky more slowly. This legend is the source of the mountain's name—Haleakala, which means "House of the Sun." The name takes on new meaning now, for the summit is a popular place in which to watch the sun rise over the clouds. You will have to rise early, for the 38-mile drive from Kahului takes about two hours, but what you will see as the sun rises over the Big Island and the Pacific, is magnificent. Sunsets are also spectacular, with a colorful light show descending on West Maui and Lanai.

Inside the park are several attractions and overlooks. The first is the Waikamoi Preserve, a nature reserve filled with North American pine, juniper, spruce, and eucalyptus, and several species of Hawaiian birds. A path leads into the preserve from Hosmer Grove on the Haleakala Crater Road.

The road also passes by several overlooks. The first is the Lelewei Overlook, about 1,200 feet below the summit. A marked trail leads into the volcano. An unusual atmospheric phenomenon is associated with this place. On certain days when the conditions are perfect, you can see yourself reflected on the clouds. This phenomenon is named the Brocken Specter, named after a similar oddity in Germany.

The next overlook is the Kalahaku Overlook at the 9,000-foot level. Near the parking lot is a protected area in which the magnificent silver sword plants grow. The plants resemble the yucca, but each sends out a stalk several feet high. Small yellow and purple flowers blossom on the stalk and the rare silver sword then dies. These plants grow in only two places in the world: next to this parking area and in the Haleakala Crater.

The next stop on the Crater Road is the Haleakala Visitors' Center. During the summer, park rangers lead tours down the paths into the crater. You can explore on your own, but be prepared either way with good hiking shoes, a poncho in case of rain, drinking water and sun lotion.

The main path into the crater is called Sliding Sands Trail. This path leads from the center into the eerie landscape that is the Haleakala Crater. The volcano last erupted in 1790, and the crater today is a quiet world of red and black earth and stones, broken only occasionally by vegetation and signs of humans. The crater is huge: 7½ miles long, 2½ miles wide, and 21 miles in circumference. It is 3,000 feet deep and covers 19 square miles.

The landscape is rugged. Smaller volcanic cones, each several hundred feet high, rise from the crater floor. The south rim is anchored by the majestic Haleakala Peak, while the east rim, the wet side of the island, slowly turns from the barren reds and blacks to the rich green of rain forest and meadows.

Beyond the Visitors' Center is the final overlook called Puu Ulaula. From this perch you can see the rest of the island, and, when conditions are perfect, every major island save Kauai. The sight is spectacular.

From this point you might see another unusual sight: bicyclists coasting down the slopes of Haleakala. The sport is popular (where else can you ride for so many miles without ever having to pedal?), and bicycles and the necessary safety equipment can be rented at several locations on the island (see Chapter 7 "Island Adventures").

After your visit to the House of the Sun, return to Highway 337 and turn left and drive two miles to the Kula Botanical Gardens. The gardens are open from 9:00 AM to 4:00 PM daily and display unusual flowers and the koa trees, whose richly colored and variegated wood is used in many fine Hawaiian crafts and furnishings.

Continue south on Highway 377 until it joins Highway 37. Take this main road for eight miles to the Tedeschi Vineyards and Winery, the only such operation in the state. Several vintages are produced here, and visitors may sample them. Try the Maui Blanc, which is a wine produced from pineapple, not grapes. The winery is located in the former jailhouse of the James Makee Ranch, where sugarcane was grown in the 1860s. The property is now the 18,000-acre Ulupalakua Ranch.

This ranch now raises cattle, not sugarcane, and if you keep watch you may see paniolos, Hawaiian cowboys, working the livestock on the range.

Retrace your drive once again on Highway 37, heading back toward Kahului. At the village of Pukalani, turn right on the Kaupakulua Road toward Makawao, a village founded by Portuguese immigrants. It's now the home of the paniolos who work the island ranches. Every Fourth of July, the Makawao Rodeo draws the cowboys for a big competition and festival.

The village is home to several interesting shops. For interesting crafts and works of art, try Goodies at 3637 Baldwin Avenue, Glassman Galleries at 3682 Makawoa Avenue, Collections at 3677 Baldwin Avenue, and Country Cupboard at 3682 Baldwin Avenue.

From this point return to Highway 37. This leads you out of the Upcountry, certainly an exotic part of an island paradise.

Wailea and Kihei

Wailea and Kihei are Maui's Gold Coast. Here are the grand resorts, the fine beaches, the beautiful golf courses, and enough tennis courts that the area calls itself Wimbledon West.

To reach this lovely region, take Highway 350 south from Kahului to the coast to Kihei Road, the main thoroughfare of this settlement. Kihei is famous for its lovely beaches. The Mai Poina Oe Iau Beach Park is popular with windsurfers, while the parks farther south—Kalama Beach, Kamaole Beach, Keawakapu—attract swimmers and snorkelers. Away from the beaches, Kihei has more than 30 condominiums, numerous restaurants, and countless shops.

Just south of this strip is the less commercial and far more elegant resort town called Wailea. Here are located the fine re-sorts—the new Four Seasons, the latest huge Hyatt, the recently refurbished Stouffer, and Inter-Continental—and the luxury villas and condos that line the landscape hills and golf courses above the shore. If elegance is what you seek, this is the place on Maui. The landscaped grounds of all the resorts and private communities are exquisite.

The four area beaches—Mokapu, Ulua, Wailea, and Polo—are great for swimming, though care should be taken when the winds are off the water and churning up the surf.

South of Wailea, the Kihei Road continues to Makena, where the Maui Prince Hotel is located. There are two fine beaches here, Big Beach and Little Beach. Unofficially, Little Beach is a nude bathing beach. But if the police catch you, you may have to go to court.

The road south of Makena is bad, passable only by four-wheel-drive vehicles. If you have such a car, continue south to the Ahihi-Kinau Natural Area Preserve, a protected area whose waters are home to more different species of fish than can be found elsewhere in the islands.

For More Information

The airports, hotels, and rental car companies have a wide variety of maps, driving guides, brochures, current-events magazines, and other publications. These are very helpful for touring the island.

For more information, contact the Maui Visitors' Bureau at 380 Diary Rd., Kahului, HI 96733 (808/871–8691) or the Maui Chamber of Commerce at 26 Puunene Ave., Kahului, HI 96733 (808/871–1111).

Festivals

Cherry Blossom Festival—A celebration of Japanese culture and heritage, with music, dance, and food featured. Late February/early March.

Buddha Day—A pageant of flowers with parades and other activities. April.

Art Maui—A celebration of the island's artists. April.

Lei Day—Celebration of the flower lei with music, hula, food, and sales of fantastic leis. May 1.

King Kamehameha Day—Parades, fairs, and other activities honor the king who united the islands. June.

Makawao Statewide Rodeo—The island's paniolos parade and then compete on July 4th.

Bon Odori Season—Buddhist festival that honors ancestors with music and dance. Late July/August.

Kapalua Music Festival—Classical music performed by top orchestras from major American cities and Tokyo.

Aloha Week—A celebration of Hawaii's culture, with music, dance, parades, crafts, food, and more. September/October.

For more information about the festivals and the exact dates, contact the visitors' information offices listed earlier.

Where to Stay

Choosing the right hotel and resort for you is not merely a matter of money. What's romantic and interesting for you may not be so for someone else. Some resorts are big and busy, with lots of organized activities. And some hotels and inns are small and low-key, preferring to leave their guests alone to enjoy the resort on their own. We feel that the resorts, hotels, and inns listed here are special places. The price breakdown we have is:

Expensive—$200 or more a night for a standard double room
Moderate—$100 to $200 a night for a standard double room
Inexpensive—Less than $100 a night for a standard double room.

At some resorts, meal plans are available that may save you money. The drawback is that the Map (Modified American Plan) restricts your flexibility in trying restaurants elsewhere.

In West Maui:

Coconut Inn—Recently transformed from a tired apartment building into a comfortable 41-room inn with spacious suites with kitchens, this hotel is one of the better bargains on the island. Facilities include a pool and spa. The beach is a half-mile away. Moderate (breakfast included). 181 Hui Rd. F, Napili, HI 96761. 808/669-5712 or 800/367-8006.

Hyatt Regency Maui—Another playground brought to you by megaresort designer Chris Hemmeter (Westin Kauai, Hyatt Regency Waikoloa, among others). Strolling flamingos, nine waterfalls, penguins, a large shopping mall, countless huge urns that look like the booty from some emperor's palace, numerous garden groves, and constant activity make this a resort for those who tire easily of their room. The 815 rooms are spacious and have recently been renovated. Facilities include a beach, golf, a huge pool, tennis, and health spa. Expensive. 200 Nohea Kai Dr., Lahaina, HI 96761. 808/667-7474 or 800/228-9000.

Kapalua Bay Hotel—This attractive resort offers 194 spacious rooms, a gardenlike setting on the beach, and enough distance from the other resorts on West Maui to make you think you have the island to yourself. Facilities include a fine beach, golf, pool, and tennis. Expensive. 1 Bay Dr., Kapalua, HI 96761. 808/669-5656 or 800/367-8000.

Maui Marriott—This is a fine resort, located between the glitter of the Hyatt and the Westin fantasy on Kaanapali beach. If you are not enamored with glitter and activities, stay at the Marriott, which has 720 large and tastefully decorated rooms and first-class service, but play—when you choose to do so—at the Hyatt and Westin. Facilities include the beach, pool, tennis, and golf. 100 Nohea Kai Dr., Lahaina, HI 96761. 808/667-1200 or 800/228-9290.

Napili Kai Beach Club—The Japanese-style rooms in this cozy resort on one of Maui's finest beaches offer a quiet retreat and a distinct change from the megaresorts. There are 137 rooms, which have Japanese decor, but not Japanese beds. Facilities include four pools, tennis, and a putting green. Expensive. 5900

Honoapiilani Highway, Lahaina, HI 96761. 808/669–6271 or 800/367–5030.

Plantation Inn—There are only nine rooms in this charming Victorian-style inn in the historic area of Lahaina. The rooms are furnished with elegant antiques. All rooms come with a private bath. Facilities include a pool. Moderate (breakfast included). 174 Lahainaluna Rd., Lahaina, HI 96761. 808/667–9225 or 800/443–6815.

Westin Maui—Another megaresort, but this one comes with a superb beach. The 762-room resort (in its previous life it was the Maui Surf) is now a wonderland of lagoons, waterfalls, flamingos, crowds, and activities. Facilities include a pool, water sports, golf, tennis, health spa, and more. Expensive. 2365 Kaanapali Parkway, Lahaina, HI 96761. 808/667–7809 or 800/228–3000.

Elsewhere on the Island:

Four Seasons Maui—The lavish new resort offers 347 spacious rooms (the bathrooms are large enough for a party), elegant gardens and terraces, and a small beach area that is usually forsaken for the magnificent pool. Other facilities include the water sports, a spa, and wonderful views. At night, the grounds are even more beautiful. Expensive. 3900 Wailea Alanui Dr., Wailea, HI 96753. 808/847–8000 or 800/332–3442.

Grand Hyatt Wailea Resort and Spa—The latest of Hyatt's megaresorts in the islands, this 787-room beachfront resort offers a huge (15,000-square-foot) pool, a 2,000-foot-long river pool with a system of locks and waterfalls, gardens, a grand spa, and more. Facilities, if you need more, include all sorts of water sports, golf, and tennis. Expensive. 3850 Wailea Alanui Dr., Wailea, HI 96753. 808/875–1234 or 800/228–9000.

Hotel Hana-Maui—Someday, if we are very, very good, we may be able to spend a week at this outstanding hotel and the 7,000-acre ranch on which it sits. One of the top resorts in the United States, Hana-Maui offers 72 spacious rooms, elegant decor, and first-class service throughout. Facilities include a beach shuttle, pool, tennis, stables, and more. Expensive, but meals are included. Hana, HI 96713. 808/536–7522 or 800/321–HANA.

Hotel Kai-Maui—This small (17 units) condo complex in Hana offers simple but comfortable rooms, a huge lava rock pool, wonderfully landscaped grounds, and a beach. Moderate. P.O. Box 38, Hana, HI 96713. 808/248–8426.

Kula Lodge—For those who hate beaches, this mountain cabin complex is great. The lodge is located in a forest and offers five rooms in two cabins (three rooms with fireplaces) as well as lovely views of the sea and mountains. Moderate. RR1, P.O. Box 475, Kula, HI 96790. 808/878–1535.

Mana Kai-Maui—Set on one of the better beaches on the island, this hotel offers 140 studio and one-bedroom apartments with or without kitchens. Facilities include the beach and pool, and rates usually include a car. Moderate. 2960 Kihei Rd., Kihei, HI 96753. 808/879–1561 or 800/525–2025.

Maui Inter-Continental Wailea—Recently renovated, this beachfront resort offers superb accommodations in a garden setting. All 560 rooms are large and tastefully decorated. The best thing about this resort is that it offers excellent rooms in a stunning setting while avoiding the circus atmosphere found elsewhere (i.e., look next door at the new Hyatt). Facilities include a beach, pool, golf, and tennis. Expensive. P.O. Box 779, Wailea, HI 96753. 808/879–1922 or 800/33–AGAIN.

Maui Prince—Secluded and stylish, this 300-room resort has fine accommodations and a sense of privacy that cannot be found in the resort strips on Maui. Facilities include a beach, pool, golf, and tennis. Expensive. 5400 Makena Alanui Dr., Kihei, HI 96753. 808/874–1111 or 800/321-MAUI.

Stouffer Wailea—Another hotel that has been renovated, this beachfront, 350-room luxury resort offers fine rooms surrounded by gardens, lagoons, and waterfalls. Facilities include a terrific beach and pool. Expensive. 3550 Wailea Alanui Dr., Wailea, HI 96753. 808/879–4900 or 800/9-WAILEA.

Wailea Villas—For those who want fully equipped luxury apartments with as many as three bedrooms, but still want beautiful grounds, a beach and pool close by, and other activities, this is the place. Expensive. 3750 Wailea Alanui Dr., Wailea, HI 96753. 808/879-1595 or 800/367-5246.

For rooms in smaller B & Bs and inns on Maui, contact Bed & Breakfast Hawaii at P.O. Box 449, Kapaa, HI 06746, or 808/ 822-7771 or 808/572-7692; Bed & Breakfast Honolulu, which has listings for Maui, at 3242 Kaohinana Dr., Honolulu, HI 96817, 800/288-4666; and Bed & Breakfast Maui-Style, at P.O. Box 886, Kihei, HI 96753, 808/879-7865 or 808/879-2352.

Where to Dine

The better restaurants on the islands are usually in the finest resorts. However, for those willing to venture outside their resort or hotel, some special dining rooms await. Always make reservations and always ask about the dress code.

The price categories for restaurants, for two persons for dinner, excluding wine, tips, and taxes, are:

Expensive—More than $75.
Moderate—$25 to $75.
Inexpensive—Less than $25.

Our Choices in West Maui:

Alex's Hole in the Wall—Wonderful Italian cooking in funky surroundings. 834 Front St., Lahaina; 808/661-3197.

Avalon—The decor is straight out of the Hawaii of the '40s, but the menu is from the '90s. It's Pacific Rim cuisine, and the marriage of the cuisines of Thailand, Mexico, California, China, and Japan is exciting. The duck and seafood dishes are the best. Expensive. 844 Front St., Lahaina. 808/667-5559.

La Bretagne—The chef is from France, and the menu at this charming country inn reflects the heritage and talent of Claude Gaty. The duck with pear and the rack of lamb are outstanding. Expensive. 562-C Front St., Lahaina. 808/661-8966.

Chez Paul—Often overlooked by those speeding by on Highway 30, this cozy (14 tables) and elegant dining room serves excellent seafood and veal dishes. Expensive. On Highway 30 one-quarter mile south of Lahaina. 808/661–3843.

Gerard's—Another French masterpiece, this dining room in the superb Plantation Inn presents some difficult choices, for the menu changes every day. If the rack of lamb or veal medallions are on it when you come, try them. Expensive. 1 Lahainaluna Rd., Lahaina. 808/661–8939.

Kapalua Bay Hotel—This resort has two fine restaurants. The Bay Club offers a setting made for romance: candles, a clifftop room with a grand view of the bay and the sunset, beautiful furnishings, and best of all, nouvelle cuisine that is among the best on the island. Stick with the fresh fish of the day. In the Plantation Veranda, the decor is more Plantation Wicker. The best dishes are the fish, particularly with saffron, and the lamb. Both restaurants are expensive. 1 Bay Dr., Kapalua. 808/669–5656.

Lahaina Treehouse—The setting really is a treehouse, the decor is casual Polynesian, and the menu is extensive and focuses on the seafood of the islands. All add up to a memorable and fun dinner. Moderate. 126 Lahainaluna Rd., Lahaina. 808/667–9224.

Longhi's—This popular casual dining room in Lahaina is renown for its fresh pasta and fish dishes, but don't overlook the sandwiches and soups, particularly the French onion soup. Moderate. 888 Front St., Lahaina. 808/667–2288.

Marco's—This slick bistro serves creative Italian dishes; winning dishes are the pastas with the fresh local seafood. Moderate. 844 Front St., Lahaina. 808/661–8877.

Mark Edison—Another romantic dining room, this restaurant has stunning views of the Iao Valley and mountains. The pasta and fish dishes are the winners here. Moderate. On the Iao Valley Road just beyond at Kepaniwai Park. 808/242–5555.

Maui Marriott—The best of the dining rooms in this resort is Lokelani, which features Maui cuisine—fresh pasta and seafood. Nikko, though, is the place to go if you want a show as well as Japanese food cooked on the teppanyaki grill. The chefs' artistry with their knives makes dinner a real treat. Both dining rooms are expensive. 100 Nohea Kai Dr., Lahaina. 808/667–1200.

Ming Yuen—Casual and plain, this local-favorite restaurant serves outstanding Cantonese dishes. Inexpensive. 162 Alamaha St., Kahului. 808/871–7787.

Siam Thai—Made famous by visiting celebrities whose pictures decorate the walls, this plain dining room serves fiery Thai cuisine. The massaman curry stew is perhaps the best and most popular of the dishes. Moderate. 123 North Market St., Wailuku. 808/244–3817.

Wailuku Grill—Very trendy decor meets imaginative chefs and the marriage is a chic dining spot serving stylish and tasty American-Italian dishes. This is a "must eat at" restaurant. Moderate. 2010 Main St., Wailuku. 808/244–7505.

Westin Maui—The best dining room in this huge resort is the lovely and romantic Sound of the Falls, which has a dance floor next to a fish pond and an island filled with flamingos, lovely views of the sunset, and excellent food. The menu is continental, but more creative than most. Expensive. 2365 Kaanapali Parkway, Lahaina. 808/667–2525.

Yori's—It's fun and funky, the food is home-style Hawaiian, and the owner is a bit camera-crazy (check out the walls of photos), but Yori's is a place you will remember long after those nouvelle dishes vanish from your brain cells. Inexpensive. 309 North Market St., Wailuku. 808/244–3121.

Elsewhere on Maui:

Four Seasons—The luxury resort has two restaurants overlooking the water. Seasons is the elegant and formal dining room, featuring island seafood with a California accent. The Pacific Grill is more casual, and the fare here is Pacific Rim and a mix of oriental dishes. Both are expensive. Wailea. 808/874–6449.

Hotel Hana-Maui—The best dining room on the island. The

menu changes nightly, offering dishes that use the best of local vegetables and seafood, emphasizing the traditions of Hawaii, Asia, and the Pacific. It's all wonderful, but, of course, what would you expect at the Hotel Hana-Maui? Expensive, but worth it. Hana. 808/248–8211.

Mama's Fish House—It isn't much on looks, but the seafood here is among the best on the island. Moderate. 799 Kaiholo Pl., Paia. 808/579–9672.

Maui Inter-Continental Wailea Hotel—La Perouse is a beautiful and intimate dining room decorated with wood paneling, antiques, and art overlooking the seacoast. Even better is the menu, which features outstanding seafood dishes, often cooked by Hawaiian methods. Expensive. Wailea. 808/879–1922.

The Prince Court—This elegant dining room features Hawaiian seafood, but the best meal is the lavish Sunday brunch, a feast certain to dissolve all dietary resolutions. Expensive, for dinner and the brunch. In the Maui Prince, 5400 Makena Alanui Dr., Makena. 808/874–1111.

Wailea Steak House—The view is wonderful: the coast below, the golf course nearby, and surrounding lovely landscaped grounds. The steaks served here are outstanding. Expensive. Wailea Iki Drive above the Wailea Shopping Village. 808/879–2875.

Luaus and Other Nightlife

The best luau is the Old Lahaina Luau, which is also the smallest but perhaps the most authentic. It's offered Tuesday, Thursday, and Saturday at a meadow near the Whaler's Marketplace in Lahaina. Call 808/667–1998. The Hyatt Regency in Kaanapali presents its "Drums of the Pacific Review" on Monday, Wednesday, Friday, and Saturday. Seating starts at 5:30 PM; call 808/661–1234, ext. 4420. The Maui Inter-Continental holds its luau on Thursday at 5:45 PM; call 808/879–1922. And the Grand Hyatt Wailea will no doubt have its own fabulous show when it finally fully opens.

HOME ON THE ISLAND RANGE

It is a surprise to many first-time visitors to the islands to discover that the largest privately owned ranch in the world isn't in Texas, but on the Big Island.

The Parker Ranch covers about 250,000 acres. It and more than 20 other large spreads make ranching a major business on the islands of Hawaii and Maui.

The ranch was created by a sailor named John Palmer Parker, who left the sea in 1809 at the age of 19 to round up stray cattle for King Kamehameha I. In time, Parker acquired his own herd, but the act that sealed his prosperity was his marriage to Kamehameha's granddaughter. In the years since, the ranch has grown and today raises an estimated 50,000 head of cattle.

The livestock is worked by paniolos (cowboys) on horseback. These cowboys can trace their heritage to three Spanish-American cowboys brought over from California by King Kamehameha III to work his herds. The islanders called them paniolos, their mispronunciation of the word Españoles (Spaniards), and the name has stuck through the years.

Each year, large rodeos on Maui and Hawaii draw hundreds of paniolos and even more visitors. The Parker Ranch Rodeo is held every July, and on Maui the Makawao Statewide Rodeo is on July 4th.

Most of the major resorts have live entertainment in the evenings. For jazz, visit Blackie's Bar, in Blackie's Boat Yard on Honoapiilani Highway in Lahaina (808/667–7979). Go early, for the entertainment stops at 8:00 PM when Blackie goes to sleep. The Crab Catcher (808/661–4423) in Whalers Village in the Kaanapali strip offers Hawaiian and contemporary music. The Molokini Lounge (808/874–1111) in the Maui Prince Hotel offers Hawaiian music and dancing most nights. And the Inu Inu

Lounge at the Maui Inter-Continental Wailea (808/879–1922) is a disco popular with a younger crowd. For more classical entertainment, the Maui Symphony Orchestra performs a number of concerts outdoors at Wailea. Call 808/244–5439.

For theater, the Maui Community Theatre (808/242–6969) presents about six plays a season in the Iao Theatre in Wailuku, and the Baldwin Theatre Guild favors musicals and comedies in its eight-play season at the Baldwin High School Theater in Kahului (808/242–5821).

For a change of pace, visit the Maui Tropical Plantation in Wailuku, where the Hawaiian Country Barbecue and Buddy Fo Revue begins with a train ride and ends with a pig-out and country/western show. Call 808/244–7643.

Exotic African and Asian animals roam wild on the Molokai Ranch Wildlife Safari. *(Hawaii Visitors Bureau; photo by William Waterfall)*

CHAPTER 5

Molokai: The Friendly Island

*M*olokai is a bit of a puzzle: How can an island so blessed with natural attractions be so often overlooked by visitors?

The fifth largest of the islands, Molokai is a place of incredible beauty. Long and narrow (37 miles by 10 miles), this 261-square-mile island offers few man-made attractions—grand resorts, gourmet restaurants, or nightlife—but makes up for it in the quiet pleasures of its undeveloped rangelands, the dramatic splendor of its northern coast, the lush jungle forests of its eastern end, and the serenity of its often-empty beaches.

The reason these wonders of nature are overlooked is explained through a story that began more than a thousand years ago, in the fifth century, when the island was first discovered by the Polynesians. Those brave explorers shunned Molokai, apparently because they thought the island was too dry to support life. The name the island bears supports this: Molo (barren) Kai (sea).

More than a thousand years later, King Kamehameha conquered the island and brought it into his realm. Still, settlers stayed away, scared away at first by the powerful Kahunas (priests who were thought to have magic powers) and later by Father Damien's leper colony at Kalaupapa on the northern shore.

By the nineteenth century, most of the island was under the control of two missionary families—Meyer and Cooke—who turned their major share of Molokai into a private ranch and plantation. This domination of Molokai scared away other settlers and businesses, preventing resort development and, as a result, preserving Molokai's natural beauty. The island remains little developed, with only 6,700 residents, one town, and not even a single traffic light.

Molokai is the creation of two major volcanoes. Maunaloa, whose dormant summit reaches a modest 1,381 feet, is the western volcano. It rules over a realm of dry, rolling grasslands. The eastern volcano is Kamakou, whose peak reaches 4,970 feet and whose rain forests support an ecological system of plants and animals found nowhere else.

The north shore's tiny peninsula of Kalaupapa has formed a third, smaller volcano called Kauhako. The coastline here is staggering: green cliffs rise more than 2,000 feet above the sea, waterfalls from rivers on the central plateau send cascades of white water down the cliff, only to disappear in clouds of mist and the sea.

Despite the fantastic scenery, Molokai may not be the island for you. It is very quiet, the major town of Kaunakakai offers few opportunities for shopping fanatics, and the resorts and restaurants are few and at a level of sophistication below those on other islands.

But if you can find beauty in an empty shore, wonder in a waterfall as tall as a Manhattan skyscraper, and romance in a place of simple charm, Molokai may be the island for your romantic getaway.

Touring the Island

Most visitors to Molokai arrive at the Hoolehau Airport, located in the center of the island, a short drive from the resort areas on the south shore and the western end of Molokai. While a driving tour of the island can be done in a day, it will require frequent retracing of your route, for there are no roads circling Molokai.

Start a tour at small Kaunakakai on the south shore. This village is a fishing and commercial port, a center of shopping and island gossip, and a place that looks like it belongs in a John Wayne western. The major attraction in town is the Kanemitsu Bakery on Ala Malama Street. Its breads, jelly rolls, doughnuts, and pies are famous throughout the island.

There are a few shops in Kaunakakai worth a stop. Molokai Island Creations, Shop 2, and the Imports Gift Shop sell interesting resort wear, jewelry, and craft items. Where are they?

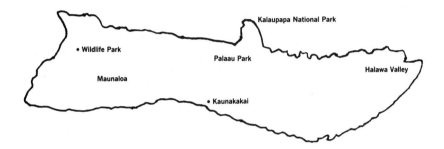

Molokai

Well, the town is so small that all you have to do to find anything is walk a few minutes along the main street and keep your eyes open.

From the village, take Highway 460 west to the Kapuaiwa Coconut Grove, a field of trees planted in the nineteenth century by Prince Lot, who later became King Kamehameha V.

Continue driving west until you reach Highway 470, then turn north and drive to Palaau State Park, 233 acres of ironwood trees and trails. At the end of the parking lot, a trail leads to the Phallic Rock, where Hawaiian women who were having trouble getting pregnant would sit, hoping the rock's powers would make them fertile. Another trail from the parking area leads to Kalaupapa Lookout, where you can get a view of the leper colony on the coast and the magnificent cliffs of the northern shore.

Another half-mile down the highway are the Kalae Stables, where a company called Rare Adventures offers a seven-hour mule ride from the stables down to the leper colony on the shore. The mule ride is safe, though a bit exciting, and there is no health danger from visiting the colony. A small number of patients still live in the colony, though no new patients are admitted.

The Rare Adventures tour includes the mule ride, a tour of the colony, and lunch. The cost is about $75 per person; call 808/552–2622 or 800/843–5978.

The northern shore is dramatically beautiful, with towering cliffs and waterfalls higher than a skyscraper, mysterious caverns, and deserted beaches. Unfortunately, the only way to see it is by boat or helicopter. (See Chapter 7, "Island Adventures.")

Another historic site is the R.W. Meyer Sugar Mill, on Route 47 between Palaau State Park and Kalaupapa. The steam-run sugar mill was built around 1878, and has been restored as a museum of that era. The mill is open from 10:00 AM to noon on Saturday and from 1:00 PM to 5:00 PM Sunday, although weekday hours are under consideration. Call 808/567–6436.

Return to Highway 460, turn west, and drive to Maunaloa. This former Dole pineapple plantation town isn't much—only a single road and a few shops run by the locals. Tao Woodcarver, the Big Wind Kite Factory, and the Molokai Red Dirt Shirt Shop are the most interesting of a very limited selection.

In Maunaloa, turn north on Kalukoi Road, which leads first to the Molokai Ranch Wildlife Safari and then to the island's major resort development, Kaluakoi Hotel and Golf Club. The Safari is a 1,000-acre game refuge that is home to more than 500 animals, including the axis deer found on many of the islands, greater kudus, elands, sable antelope, and other exotic species from Africa and Asia.

Tours of the refuge are made on vans that depart from the Kaluakoi Resort just down the road. (Call 808/552–2555.) The resort is the largest on the island, combining a hotel, condos, and the island's only golf course.

Beyond the resort on Highway 460 is Papohaku Beach, three miles of beautiful, unspoiled white sand. The water can be rough in the winter months, so check first on the conditions before swimming.

Return east on Highway 460 to Kaunakakai and drive east on Highway 450 for six miles to the Kalokoeli Fish Pond, an aquaculture operation built in the thirteenth century.

Drive another six miles to Kamalo, a small port where you can see St. Joseph's Church, a tiny chapel built in 1876 by Father Damien, the priest who ministered to the lepers.

North of you in the mountainous interior is the Kamakou Preserve, 2,700 rugged acres filled with exotic plants, trees, animals, and birds. There are no roads to the preserve, and only about 12 guided hikes are held each year. Call 808/567–6680 for the date and time of the next hike.

Another five-mile drive brings you to the ancient Iliiliopae Heiau (temple). Park at the sign indicating the Wailau Trail and walk into the mountains for ten minutes until you come to the huge (300-foot-long) temple. This is an important shrine to Hawaiians. Human sacrifices were held here, and some islanders still believe the shrine holds magical power.

By now the coastal scenery has changed from a craggy lava-rock shore to empty white-sand beaches. Continue driving through the now-twisting road until you come to the Halawa Valley Overlook. The scene is incredible: a lush jungle valley guarded by steep cliffs, two waterfalls plunging down the cliffs and disappearing into the lush jungle floor, and beyond these sights, the sea.

This valley was home to some of the first Hawaiians. Ruins have been found and dated back to 650 AD. The valley was farmed until 1946 when a terrible tidal wave destroyed the village here.

Follow the road down to the church and park. From here a trail leads to the Moaula Falls, a 250-foot-high torrent that empties into a lovely pool that is picture-perfect for swimming.

For More Information

The airports, hotels, and rental car companies have a wide variety of maps, driving guides, brochures, current-events magazines, and other publications. They are very helpful for touring the island. For more information, contact the Destination Molokai Association at P.O. Box 1067, Kaunakakai, HI 96748. 808/567-6255.

Festivals

Molokai is very quiet and small. Though the islanders celebrate these festivals, don't expect a major show of it.

Cherry Blossom Festival—A celebration of Japanese culture and heritage, with music, dance, and food featured. Late February/early March.

Buddha Day—A pageant of flowers with parades and other activities. April.

Lei Day—Celebration of the flower lei with music, hula, food, and sales of fantastic leis. May 1.

King Kamehameha Day—Parades and fairs along with other activities honor the king who united the islands. June.

Bon Odori Season—Buddhist festival that honors ancestors with music and dance. Late July/August.

MARK TWAIN ON HAWAII

"No alien land in all the world has any deep, strong charm for me but that one; no other land could so longingly and beseechingly haunt me sleeping and waking, through half a lifetime, as that one has done. Other things leave me, but it abides; other things change, but it remains the same. For me its balmy airs are always blowing, its summer seas flashing in the sun; the pulsing of its surf beat is in my ear; I can see its garlanded craigs, its leaping cascades, its plumy palms drowsing by the shore; its remote summits floating like islands above the cloudrack; I can feel the spirit of its woodland solitude; I can hear the plash of its brooks; in my nostrils still live the breath of flowers that perished twenty years ago."

—Mark Twain, 1866

Aloha Week—A celebration of Hawaii's culture, with music, dance, parades, crafts, food, and more. September/October.

Molokai-to-Oahu Canoe Race—The major event on the island, taking place in September.

For more information about the festivals and the exact dates, contact the visitors' information offices listed earlier.

Where to Stay

The good news about finding accommodations on Molokai is that the rates are about half that of rooms on other islands. The bad news is that there aren't many choices.

Choosing the right hotel and resort for you is not merely a matter of money. What's romantic and interesting for you may not be so for someone else. Some resorts are big and busy, with lots of organized activities. And some hotels and inns are small and low-key, preferring to leave their guests alone to enjoy the resort on their own. We feel that the resorts, hotels, and inns listed here are special places. The price breakdown we have is as follows:

> *Expensive*—$100 or more a night for a standard double room
> *Moderate*—$50 to $100 a night for a standard double room
> *Inexpensive*—Less than $50 a night for a standard double room.

At some resorts, meal plans are available that may save you money. The drawback is that the Map (Modified American Plan) restricts your flexibility in trying restaurants elsewhere.

Our Favorite Hotels, Inns, and Resorts:

Hotel Molokai—This Polynesian-style beachfront hotel offers 56 rooms in small, multiroom cottages that can best be described as rustic and laid-back. The beach is so-so: the water is too shallow here. Facilities include a pool. Moderate. P.O. Box 546, Kaunakakai, HI 96748. 808/553-5347 or 800/922-7866.

Kaluakoi Hotel and Golf Club—The largest resort on the island, this resort offers 289 lovely rooms in thatched cottage complexes scattered around the beautifully landscaped grounds. Facilities include kitchenettes, pool, beach, tennis, and golf. Expensive. Maunaloa, HI 06770. 808/552-2555 or 800/367-6046.

Ke Nani Kai—There are 120 spacious apartments with tropical decor in this condo complex next to the Kaluakoi Hotel and the west shore beaches. Facilities include pool, spa, tennis, and a beach five minutes' walk away. Expensive. Maunaloa, HI 96770. 808/552-2761 or 800/922-7866.

Paniolo Hale—The excellent condo complex has 77 one- and two-bedroom apartments, all with great views of the gardens or the ocean. The location is perfect for scenery lovers: the golf course is next door, the site is a bluff overlooking the beach, and the gardens are pleasant. Expensive. P.O. Box 146, Maunaloa, HI 96770. 808/552-2731 or 800/367-2984.

Where to Dine

Dining choices are very limited on Molokai. The price categories for restaurants, for two persons for dinner, excluding wine, tips, and taxes, are:

Expensive—More than $75.
Moderate—$25 to $75.
Inexpensive—Less than $25.

Our Choices on the Island:

Hop Inn—Delicious Chinese food, and plenty of it, at this very plain restaurant in Kaunakakai. Try the lemon chicken or the sweet and sour dishes, and don't be put off by the slightly shabby decor. Inexpensive. Ala Malama St. 808/553-5465.

Hotel Molokai—The main dining room here is called the Holo Kai. The location is beachfront, the decor is Polynesian, and the food can be quite good, particularly at breakfast when the crepes, French toast, and pancakes are served. Dinner is more traditional, featuring seafood and the local favorite of beef stew. Both are good choices. Moderate. 808/553-5347.

JoJo's Cafe—This cafe looks more like a saloon, with its nineteenth century bar and old booths. The food is excellent, with local fish, ribs, and steaks the best choices. Inexpensive. Maunaloa. 808/552-2803.

Mid-Nite Inn—The decor isn't much—lots of Naugahyde, linoleum, and Formica—but the menu promises "The Best Fish Served Anywhere." While the inn falls a bit short of that claim, the seafood dishes are excellent. Try the fried opakapaka and the mahimahi in soy sauce. Inexpensive. Ala Malama St., Kaunakakai. 808/553-5302.

Kaluakoi Hotel and Golf Club—This resort's Ohia Lodge is the closest thing there is to a gourmet dining experience on Molokai. This restaurant promises a lot, but stay away from the more creative and challenging dishes. Barbecued chicken, fresh fish, and steak are sound selections. Expensive. 808/552-2555.

Nightlife

We said it was a quiet island, but it isn't so quiet that you can't find some live music. The Hotel Molokai (808/553–5347) and the Pau Hana Inn (808/553–5342) in Kaunakakai and in the Kaluakai Hotel and Golf Club (808/552–2555) on the island's west end have live music—usually Hawaiian folk—most weekends.

Diamond Head, beyond the Waikiki resort beach, is one of the most recognizable scenes in the world. *(Hawaii Visitors Bureau)*

CHAPTER 6

Oahu: The Gathering Place

*F*ormed by two volcanic ridges but shaped forever in our minds by images of a world-famous beach and a few hours of infamy, Oahu is the most familiar of all the Hawaiian islands.

On Oahu you can find the familiar touchstones of twentieth century America: corporate headquarters, high-rise buildings, huge shopping malls, ethnic neighborhoods, expressways, and traffic jams. Oahu has 830,600 residents—more than three-fourths of all the residents of the state. Half of those 830,600 live in Honolulu, a tourist mecca that attracts more than 3 million visitors a year. These visitors are crammed into Honolulu and the resort area of Waikiki on the south side of the 608-square-mile island.

Oahu was created 4 to 6 million years ago by two volcanic mountain ranges joined by a plateau formed by erosion over the centuries. The two mountain ranges—the Waianae Mountains on the west that rise as much as 4,000 feet and the Koolau Mountains to the east that soar to about 3,000 feet—dominate the 40-mile by 26-mile boot-shaped island. In the centuries since, the mountain ranges have been sculpted and carved into dramatically beautiful valleys and ridges. The plateau between the mountains is a fertile agricultural plain where bananas, pineapples, and vegetables are grown on large plantations.

Oahu wasn't always the center of Hawaiian power and wealth. King Kamehameha conquered Oahu in 1795, but he and his successors maintained their rule of the island empire from the Big Island until the mid-nineteenth century, when they finally moved the throne to Honolulu. Since then, Honolulu has been the seat of government for the monarchy, the republic, the territory, and finally, the state.

But neither the monarchy, the mountains, nor the fertile plateau shaped the future of Oahu and Hawaii as much as two harbors on the island's south shore. The arrival of Europeans in the nineteenth century turned Honolulu's harbor into a thriving port for whalers, fur merchants, and other sea traders. Just west of this small harbor was a giant bay, protected by a small inlet and broken into three arms by peninsulas and a large island. More than a century ago, U.S. military strategists envisioned the huge anchorage as a vital link in the American drive for Manifest Destiny, and turned the harbor into a mighty naval base.

It is on this southern shore of Oahu that Hawaii became firmly fixed in the consciousness of mainland America. The image of America's Pacific fleet burning in the harbor after a surprise attack by the Japanese on December 7, 1941, remains vivid even a half-century later. Another image, far more romantic and desirable, is shaped by a long dormant volcanic crater called Diamond Head and the adjacent beach known throughout the world as Waikiki.

Waikiki is a beautiful crescent of white sand and swaying palms. Unlike other popular beaches, Waikiki is also an electrifying carnival, a resort that sizzles with excitement, elegance, and crowds of visitors.

The frenzy found in Waikiki often overshadows other attractions on Oahu, which has just as much natural beauty as its sister islands. Steep ravines coated with lush vegetation, isolated beaches, quaint coastal towns, and the burial tombs of kings can be found not far from the wonders of Waikiki.

Touring Oahu is different than sightseeing on the other islands. While those tours are almost all by car, the main sights on Oahu can be seen on walking or driving tours. We have broken Oahu into four tours: Two walking tours—Honolulu and Waikiki—and two driving tours—East Oahu (from Diamond Head around the windward eastern and northern shores before returning through the central Plateau) and the Waianae Coast, an area often overlooked by visitors that remains the most unspoiled part of the island.

Getting around Honolulu is also possible by bus. The Waikiki Trolley, an open-air bus made to resemble the San Francisco trolleys, offers guided tours. Call 808/526–0112. The Bus, Oahu's

Waimea

Laie

Haleiwa

Kaaawa

East Oahu

Koolau Mountains

Waianae Mountains

Makaha

Kahaluu

Waianae Coast

Pearl Harbor

Honolulu

Waikiki

Hanauma Bay

Diamond Head

Koko Head

Oahu

mass transit system, offers efficient service to all the urban sights as well as most of the towns outside Honolulu. Call 808/536–1611 for route information.

Millions of visitors come to Hawaii each year, and most of them spend some time on Oahu, even if it's only to catch a flight to another island. Those who never leave the airport miss out on the vital nature of Oahu. If there is one island that should be explored by all, Oahu is the one. For of all the islands, only Oahu has it all: natural beauty, vibrant nightlife, miles of beaches, magnificent resorts, and the sense of being the heartbeat of Hawaii.

Honolulu

The heart of Hawaii can be found in the Iolani Palace, at King and Richard streets. The majestic Victorian palace was built by King David Kalakaua and served as the official residence of Hawaii's regents until 1893, when the monarchy was overthrown.

The palace has been restored, and the one-hour tours go through the throne room, dining room, the king's library, and other parts of the four-story palace. The palace furnishings are replicas, though, because most of the furnishings were sold after the ouster of the ruling family. The tours are offered from 9:00 AM to 2:15 PM, Wednesday through Saturday. Reservations are required; call 808/522–0832.

Other attractions on the palace grounds include the Kalakaua Coronation Bandstand, an octagonal pavilion where the Royal Hawaiian Band plays at noon on most Fridays, and the Iolani Barracks, where the Palace Guards once lived. The barracks, built in 1871, serves as the ticket office for palace tours and a gift shop, but plans are to convert it into a military museum.

From the palace, walk out the east palm-shaded driveway to the State Capitol, an unusual building that is meant to unite symbolically the main elements of the islands: (vegetation) the concrete columns supporting the office balconies are shaped like royal palms; (volcanoes) the two legislative chambers are conical, like volcanoes; (ocean) the reflecting pool. Sculptures, tapestries, koa wood panelling, and furnishings make this government building a fascinating and beautiful stop.

Cross behind the Capitol to 320 S. Beretania Street, where you will find Washington Place, a Greek Revival Home built in 1846 by a sea captain. The mansion was the home of Queen Liliuokalani after she was deposed in 1893. In 1922, the government bought the mansion and made it the home of the governor.

A block north at Queen Emma Square are St. Andrew's Cathedral, a structure begun by the Episcopal diocese in 1867, consecrated in 1902, but not finished until 1958. The cathedral mixes classic designs with Hawaiian floral decorations.

The square itself was a park created by King Kamehameha IV in 1858. Only the huge Moreton Bay fig tree, a garden pool, and a terra cotta bust of Queen Emma remain of this once-fine park.

On the other side of the palace grounds, out the western driveway, is the statue of Kamehameha the Great, a duplicate of the one at Kapaau on the Big Island. The statue marks the centennial of Captain Cook's discovery of the islands. The original statue was lost at sea, and a second casting was ordered from American sculptor Thomas Gould before the original was discovered. This second casting was placed in Honolulu before the Aliiolani Hale (Judiciary Building) in 1883, five years later, while the recovered original was placed on the Big Island near where it was found.

From the statue, walk south on King Street one block to Punchbowl Street. At 957 Punchbowl Street is the Kawaiahao Church, a structure of wood and coral built in 1842 on the site of Hawaii's first mission. The church has been the setting for royal weddings, funerals, and other major events. King Lunalilo is buried in the tomb on the church grounds.

Just behind the church is the Adobe School House at 872 Mission Lane. Missionaries built the school in 1835.

Return to King Street and continue walking south to 553

King Street and the Mission Houses Museum, where you can take a guided tour of three houses that contain exhibits of the first missionaries to the islands. The houses include: a white frame house, prefabricated in Boston and shipped in 1821; a coral-stone house built in 1841; and a two-story, coral-stone house built in 1831 by Levi Chamberlain, the business manager of the mission. Tours are given on the hour from 9:00 AM to 4:00 PM daily; call 808/531–0481.

Across King Street are three red-and-white, Georgian-style buildings built between 1820 and 1848 by the Congregational Churches of the islands as memorials for their missionaries. These buildings are now government offices.

Another building honoring the early missionaries is at 560 Kawaiahao Street, where the Mission Historical Library holds a collection of the books, pamphlets, and manuscripts of the Hawaiian Mission Children's Society and the Hawaii Historical Society.

These attractions make up the historical area of Honolulu. To continue a tour of Honolulu, walk south on Richards Street next to the Iolani Palace down to Ala Moana Boulevard and turn right. Continue walking about a third of a mile until you come to the busy waterfront and Pier 7. Turn right and go to the Hawaii Maritime Center, which features the four-masted Falls of Clyde, a nineteenth century square-rigger used as a museum; the Kalakaua Boat House, a museum devoted to whaling and the history of Honolulu Harbor; Hokule'a, a pavilion where a 60-foot replica of the double-hulled seagoing canoes used by the Polynesians is displayed; and the Aloha Tower, which has a ninth-floor museum and a tenth-floor observatory offering striking views of the city and shore.

After viewing these colorful sights along the waterfront, walk away from the water on Fort Street, which turns into a pedestrian mall with shops, restaurants, new buildings and old. It's a lively area dotted with small parks perfect for a brief stop.

A few blocks north is Chinatown, an area bordered by Nuuanu Avenue, Beretania Street, the Nuuanu Stream, and the waterfront. Though no longer the residential center of the island's Chinese immigrants, the area remains the cultural, financial, and social mecca of the Chinese as well as many of the more recent immigrants, like the Vietnamese and Filipinos.

Walking tours of Chinatown are offered by the Chinese Chamber of Commerce Tour, at 42 N. King Street (808/533–3181). The tour goes to such places as a former opium den, the street markets, and a temple.

The Oahu Market at King and Kekaulike streets in Chinatown is an open-air bazaar where fresh fruits and vegetables are hawked daily along with more unusual items like pumpkin blossoms, crispy duck, taro leaves, and seafood delicacies. Opposite the market in the L. Ah Leong Building is a marketplace where Vietnamese, Filipino, and other recent immigrants sell their food and wares. Both markets are open daily.

Several other sights near downtown Honolulu will require a car to visit. The Bishop Museum and Planetarium, a world-famous center of Polynesian history and culture, is at 1525 Bernice Street. The museum is open from 9:00 AM to 5:00 PM Monday through Saturday and on the first Sunday of the month. On those Sundays, the museum holds a day of activities and entertainment. Call 808/847–3511.

Oahu's gardens are also famous. The Foster Botanic Gardens at 180 N. Vineyard Boulevard has 20 acres of unusual and beautiful trees, orchids and "prehistoric" plants. It's open from 9:00 AM to 4:00 PM daily. Call 808/533–3214. The Moanaloa Gardens at 1401 Mahiole features striking monkeypod trees, streams, koi ponds, a Victorian cottage built for Kamehameha V and a wood party pavilion. It's open from 8:00 AM to 4:00 PM weekdays. Call 808/833–1944.

The pristine white memorial that stands guard over the sunken USS Arizona at the U.S. Naval Base at Pearl Harbor is a moving sight. You can view a 20-minute documentary on the attack, tour the visitor center exhibits and take a shuttle boat out to the memorial, which sits atop the sunken battleship. The memorial is open from 8:00 AM to 3:00 PM, Tuesday–Sunday. Call 808/422–0561.

VALLEY OF THE KINGS

Nuuanu Valley is Hawaii's equivalent of Egypt's valley of the kings. The valley, north of Honolulu Harbor not far from the bustle of downtown Honolulu, is the site of the Royal Mausoleum, where six of Hawaii's eight monarchs are buried. The mausoleum at 2261 Nuuanu Avenue was built in 1862 by King Kamehameha IV and Queen Emma.

Buried in the tomb are Liholiho, Kauikeaouli, Alexander Liholiho and Lot (respectively, Kamehameha II through V), and David Kalakaua and Queen Liliuokalani. King David William Lunalilo is buried on the grounds of the Kawaiahao Church at King and Punchbowl streets in downtown Honolulu.

The burial site of the most famous of all islanders—King Kamehameha I, the ruler who united all the islands—is a mystery. After his death in 1819, the islands' highest chiefs took his body to a secret place for burial. It has never been found. According to island legend, "The morning star alone knows where Kamehameha's bones are guarded."

The final attraction near Honolulu can be seen by taking Nuuanu Avenue into the hills. In this lovely, rugged valley are historic churches and some grand mansions. The sight we feel you should see is at 2261 Nuuanu Avenue—the Royal Mausoleum, the burial ground of six of the island's eight monarchs.

Waikiki

Seeking a serene spot to spend a few days to soak up the sun and enjoy the ocean? If so, Waikiki is definitely not the place for you.

The world-famous resort is anything but quiet. Its streets and hotels are bustling with masses of visitors searching endlessly for something—jewelry, art, fine clothing, gourmet dinners, exciting nightlife, or a new love. And the beaches are more of the same, a daily carnival where outrigger canoes, catamarans, surfers, ESPN water-sports contests, and swimmers compete for space and attention with sun worshippers, Frisbee throwers, bands, dancers, beachcombers, and a few brave souls stretched out on towels.

Waikiki blends the best and worst of all resorts. The resort area covers only one square mile, and on the average day about 60,000 visitors join the 50,000 residents and workers in filling its streets and attending its attractions. The traffic is often a horror, almost every place is crowded, and the noise can be irritating. But Waikiki is also electrifying, a place where you go to recharge your batteries and get your adrenalin racing, a place where it is all too easy to break those resolutions: just a few more shops, just one more "Tiny Bubbles" crooned by Don Ho, and just one more drink sipped while sitting under the beautiful banyan tree on the oceanfront patio at the Moana.

Waikiki is many things, but more often, it is misunderstood. This resort is actually a small peninsula—about two miles long and no more than a half-mile wide—formed by the ocean and the Ali Wai Canal. And Waikiki Beach is actually a series of crescent beaches that have their own names—Duke Kahanamoku, Kuhio, Kahaloa, Ulukou, Queen's Surf, Sans Souci, and Grays.

A walking tour of this magnificent, maddening playground should start on the western end at the Hilton Hawaiian Village, 2005 Kalia Road, a huge (2,522 rooms) resort built in the 1950s. The Rainbow Tower at the village is decorated with 30-story murals, and the beach here is named Duke Kahanamoku after Hawaii's famous Olympic swimming champion.

Walk east on Kalia Road to Saratoga Road where, at No. 245, you will find the Urasenke Foundation of Hawaii Tea Room. From 10:00 AM to noon, Wednesdays and Fridays, kimono-clad Japanese perform an elaborate tea ceremony which you can take part in for a small donation.

Walk away from the water on Saratoga until you come to

Kalakaua Avenue, the main thoroughfare of Waikiki. Turn right and walk three blocks to the Royal Hawaiian Shopping Center, a three-building complex connected by bridges at 2201 Kalakaua Avenue, next to the famed pink palace of the Royal Hawaiian Hotel. Here you will find world-famous boutiques like Chanel and Louis Vuitton as well as the Little Hawaiian Craft Shop, the Friendship Store operated by the People's Republic of China, other shops, and restaurants.

This shopping center also hosts a number of free demonstrations of Hawaiian culture, including lei making, hula lessons, Hawaiian quilting, songs, and dances. The shows are at 10:30 AM Monday, Wednesday, and Friday, at 9:30 AM Tuesday and Thursday, and at 10 AM Saturday.

Across the street at 2270 Kalakaua Avenue is the Waikiki Shopping Center, another complex of shops and food outlets. The fourth floor showroom is where the free hula show "Waikiki Calls" is held at 6:30 PM and 8:00 PM every day but Sunday.

Before continuing east, take time to stroll through the lobby and around the grounds of the Royal Hawaiian Hotel, the pink palace at 2259 Kalakaua Avenue. This lovely hotel was built in 1927 and remains a gracious and elegant oasis in busy Waikiki.

Another block east of the Royal Hawaiian, on the land side of Kalakaua Avenue, is a truly bizarre bazaar—the International Marketplace. It's a two-level, open-air circus crammed with shops, vendors, and kiosks selling every possible permutation of Hawaiian handicraft and souvenir, most of the items forgettable.

Cross the avenue again to the seaside and walk to the stately, ivory-colored Sheraton Moana Surfrider. The Moana—the restored Victorian centerpiece built in 1901 that now stands flanked by two modern towers—is an elegant stop for tea or a drink under the spreading banyan tree in the beachside court. Next to the hotel on the sea side are the Wizard Stones of Waikiki, two huge boulders that legend says were placed in honor of four prophets who came to Hawaii from Tahiti in the fifteenth century.

Another block toward Diamond Head is the Pacific Beach Hotel, whose three-story, 280,000-gallon aquarium is fascinating. Divers feed the fish several times a day, and you can watch from the lobby or the restaurants on the upper floors.

The beach in this part of Waikiki is a show. Catamarans, outrigger canoes, beach games, and the see-and-be-seen crowd compete for attention on this strand. It you want lots of activity, with your own piece of sand, spend a few hours here.

At the eastern end of the beach is Kapiolani Park, a 170-acre oasis from the Waikiki frenzy that offers a zoo, aquarium, bandstand, tennis, archery, and golf driving range. The Honolulu Zoo is open from 8:30 AM to 4:30 PM daily, and holds 900 different animals on its 43 acres. The Waikiki Aquarium is open from 9:00 AM to 5:00 PM daily and holds some interesting specimens of the underwater world.

Beyond the park is the volcanic crater called Diamond Head. Formed about 150,000 years ago, the crater got its name from sailors who thought the crystals found on its slopes were diamonds.

You can drive around the crater by taking Diamond Head Road from the park. The road will take you to some stunning views of Honolulu. A tunnel leading off Diamond Head Road near 18th Avenue will take you into the crater. The inside is much less attractive than the outside of Diamond Head. The vast basin is empty except for a National Guard base and a Federal Aviation Administration air traffic control center.

The crater road is open from 6:00 AM to 6:00 PM daily. If you drive into the crater, look for a path leading up to the seaside rim of the crater. The climb is a bit demanding, but the views from the rim are outstanding.

East Oahu

Travelling around Oahu's windward shore requires making some decisions: Should you make the loop tour of the southeastern tip around Koko Head? Or should you bypass Koko and take the Pali Highway through the Koolau Mountains to the eastern shore and then go north before returning to Honolulu by the central plateau?

It all depends on how much time you have. Koko Head is Oahu's finest residential area, a region of grand homes, gorgeous scenery, isolated beaches, and a marine park. Making the circle tour of this area will take about a half-day. Start it by taking Kahala Avenue where Diamond Head Road turns away from the sea. This magnificent boulevard exudes style, class, and money: lavish mansions (some selling for more than $10 million), majestic trees, and beautiful gardens line the roadside. At road's end is the superb Kahala Hilton, the finest resort on the island. It's a must-stop, if only to see the dolphins, sea turtles, and a wide variety of colorful ocean fishes swimming in the hotel's lagoons. These sea creatures are fed every day at 11:00 AM, 2:00 PM and 4:00 PM.

Return on Kahala Avenue to Kealaolu Avenue, turn right, and drive to Kalanianaole Highway (Highway 72), then turn right again. On your left are the rugged ridges and valleys of the Koolaus, while on your right is the ocean, hidden occasionally by houses and other development. The biggest development is Hawaii Kai, a vast residential area that combines homes with golf courses, a marina, and shopping centers. Pass by Hawaii Kai to Koko Head Regional Park, an undeveloped area offering fine beaches, scenic overlooks, and beautiful scenery.

One of the most beautiful spots on Oahu is Hanauma Bay. The horseshoe-shaped bay is picture-perfect, the beach is small but usually uncrowded, and the waters are great for swimming and snorkeling.

A bit farther on the highway is the Blowhole Lookout, which offers a view of the Halana Blowhole, a lave tube that creates a geyser when the waves hit it at the right angle. The blowhole is fickle, hostage to the tides, winds, and currents, and may not put on its show when you stop. The sandy beach nearby is beautiful but the waters are usually too dangerous to swim. The beach is also known by locals as "Eternity Beach," for it was the beach used in the steamy passion-in-the-surf scene in the movie *From Here to Eternity.*

Continue driving east and then north on Highway 72 to the Sea Life Park, a theme park displaying several thousand forms of sea life. Dolphins, whales, and sea lions star in shows here, and the 300,000-gallon aquarium is home to more than 2,000 different sea creatures. The Pacific Whaling Museum next to the park has fascinating exhibits on whaling in the islands. The park and museum are open daily from 9:30 AM to 5:00 PM Mondays–Wednesdays and Saturdays, 9:30 AM to 10:00 PM Thursdays, Fridays, and Sundays.

Several beaches close to the park offer fine sunbathing and swimming when conditions are right. Makapuu Beach Park, across from Sea Life Park, is popular with body surfers. Waimanalo Bay has several beaches, but the water can be rough. And Kailua Beach Park, on the edge of Kailua, is popular with windsurfers and boaters.

Continue driving north on Highway 72 until you come to the Pali Highway (Highway 61) and turn left to return to Honolulu and Waikiki.

The second tour around Oahu's windward coast also starts on Highway 61, where it joins Highway H1 in Honolulu. The Pali Highway is a dramatic road cutting across the Koolau Mountains, passing through tunnels entering nearly vertical cliffs before passing by the Pali Lookout, a spot with a scenic view of the windward shore, and then intersecting with Highway 83, the main route to the northern shore. This drive takes you past some of the finest surfing beaches in the world, countless miles of dramatic coastline, and some interesting towns and historic sites.

So, from Highway 61, turn left (north) on Highway 83 and continue north past Kaneohe and its adjacent bay, a body of water popular with boaters. Two miles north of town on the right is the Heeia Fishpond, a massive (88 acres) pond built by ancient Hawaiians. The pond is so large that it is better to drive past it to the Heeia State Park, where the overlook at Kealohi Point offers a better view of the old structure.

From the park, drive north to Kahaluu and stop at Senator Fong's Plantation and Gardens. These gardens consist of five valleys and plateaus named after the five presidents Senator Hiram Fong served under in Washington. The gardens are lush, and the pond and nearby Koolaus make this a beautiful stop for photographs.

After the gardens, drive another mile north to Kahekili Highway and turn left. Drive south a bit more than a mile to the Byodo-In Temple, a replica of Kyoto's classic temple of the same name on a spectacular site between a carp-filled pond and the stately mountains. Continue south on Kahekili Highway another mile-plus to Haiku Gardens, a lush park with bamboo groves, carp ponds, and grass houses.

After visiting these sights, retrace your drive back to Highway 83 and continue north. The highway enters the verdant farming area of Oahu, and the numerous fruit and vegetable stands along the road offer many reasons to stop and pick up a snack for the trip.

At the north end of Kaneohe Bay is Kualoa Regional Park, a historic area featuring more ancient fish ponds, remains of a sugar mill, and other scenic views.

North of this park, Highway 83 begins to pass by more beach parks—Kaaawa, Swanzy, and Kahana Bay. The latter is the best of the three, with shallow, safe waters, a shaded beach area, and beautiful views of the nearby banana and mango plantations.

North of the beaches is the small town of Hauula, where you can follow signs to Sacred Falls, a picturesque, 80-foot torrent at the head of the Kaliuwaa Valley. It's a two-mile walk from the parking area on the highway just south of town, but worth it if you have the time and energy.

North of Hauula is Laie, a town created in 1864 by Mormons. The campus of Brigham Young University-Hawaii is here, as well as the Polynesian Cultural Center, a park that recreates the villages of Fiji, Hawaii, the Marquesas, Maori, New Zealand, Tahiti, Samoa, and Tonga. You can take a walking tour of the park or ride in outrigger canoes. What you will see are recreated villages; demonstrations of Polynesian crafts, music, and dances; and elaborate floor shows and Polynesian reviews (see "Luaus and Other Nightlife" at the end of the chapter).

From Laie, Highway 83 turns west as it passes the Turtle Bay Hilton and then Sunset Beach, where the famous Banzai Pipeline of 30-foot waves hits the shore every winter. The waves are as fascinating as they are dangerous, and only the most daring and experienced surfers dare challenge them.

Beyond the beach is Waimea Falls Park, where you can walk or ride a minibus on the one mile trip to the 45-foot falls. At 11:00 AM, 12:30 PM, 2:00 PM, and 3:30 PM, cliffdivers take the 50-foot plunge from above the falls into the pool below. For romance, try the one-hour walks during the full moon. Call 808/ 638–8511.

The 1,800-acre park also hosts exhibits on such ancient Hawaiian games as ulu maika, a form of lawn bowling (you can try your hand at them), a burial temple, and gardens. Trails lead out into the lush landscape of the park and its exotic vegetation and roaming birdlife.

Just past the park is Waimea Beach, the strand made famous in the Beach Boys' old song "Surfin' U.S.A." In the winter, the waves here can reach 25 feet, and the waters are only for the expert surfers. During the summer, however, the waters are calm and are perfect for swimming.

Highway 83 continues west, passing through the old plantation town of Haleiwa and its nice beach park. In Haleiwa, turn left (south) on Kamehameha Highway (Highway 99) and enter Oahu's central plateau.

The plateau is 1,000 feet above sea level and is home to the island's largest pineapple and sugarcane plantations. The Dole Pineapple Pavilion, on Kamehameha Highway about seven miles south of Haleiwa, and the adjacent Helemano Plantation and Del Monte Variety Garden, display and sell the fruits of labor. The Poamoho Village next to these stops is an old plantation camp.

A bit further south on Kamehameha Highway are the Kukaniloko Birth Stones (watch for a dirt road turnoff opposite Whitemore Avenue). On these stones were born many members of Hawaii's royal family.

The next town on the main highway is Wahiawa, a quiet

town whose main street is lined with turn-of-the-century wooden structures gaily decorated in pastel tones. The Wahiawa Botanic Gardens at 1396 California Avenue exhibits plants that thrive in wet, upland plateaus. The gardens are open 9:00 AM to 4:00 PM daily.

From Wahiawa you can take Highway 99 west to Schofield Barracks, the military base that was the setting for *From Here to Eternity*, or take Highway 80 into downtown Honolulu.

The Waianae Coast

Usually bypassed by visitors to Oahu, the leeward Waianae Coast is a region of small plantation towns, uncrowded beaches with calm waters, ancient temples, and often spectacular views of the Waianae Mountains and valleys.

To reach this shore, take Highway H1 west from Honolulu. Turn south on Fort Weaver Road (Highway 76) and visit Ewa, a small and colorful plantation town built by the Ewa Sugar Company in the 1920s.

Return to Highway H1 and continue west, passing around the Waianae Mountains and continuing north on Highway 93. This coastal road takes you past numerous fine beach parks—from south to north, Kahe Point, Nanakuli, Ulehawa, Maili, Laulualei, Pokai Bay, Waianae, Mauna Lahilahi, Makaha, and Keaau—and a few colorful seaport towns.

The most interesting towns are Waianae, where a cultural center in the Waianae Shopping Mall offers exhibits and guided tours on the historic sites on this coast, and Makaha, the surfing center of the leeward shore. Surfing contests are held there often in the winter months.

Near Makaha is the Kaneaki Heiau, a temple built around 1535 and used for nearly three centuries. To see it, take the Makaha Valley Road to the Sheraton Makaha Resort, turn left and then right before the tennis courts and then right again. The temple is open daily from 10:00 AM to 2:00 PM, but you will have to ask permission from the Sheraton to visit the temple.

From this temple, located in a lush valley between two Waianae ridges reaching from the mountain crest to the sea, the busy streets of Waikiki seem a world away.

For More Information

The airports, hotels, and rental car companies have a wide variety of maps, driving guides, brochures, current-events magazines, and other publications. They are very helpful for touring the island.

The Hawaiian Visitors' Bureau at 2270 Kalakaua Avenue in Waikiki has a lot of information about island tours, activities, attractions, and current events. You can call them at 808/923–1811 or write them at 2270 Kalakaua Ave., Eighth Floor, Honolulu, HI 96815. The bureau is open 8:00 AM to 4:30 PM, weekdays.

Festivals

'40s Big Band Music and Dancing—Every Monday from 2:00 PM to 4:00 PM at the Waikiki Community Center.

Hula Bowl—All-star college football classic. January.

International Bodyboard Championships—Two days of surfing on the Banzai Pipeline on the north shore. Mid-January.

Narcissus Festival—A celebration of the Chinese New Year with parades, cooking demonstrations, and a street festival in Chinatown. Late January.

NFL Pro Bowl—The top NFL players meet. February.

Hawaiian Mardis Gras—Dancing, music, and a carnival in Honolulu. Late February.

Cherry Blossom Festival—A celebration of Japanese culture and heritage, with music, dance, and food featured. Late February/early March.

Hawaiian Honohono Exotic Orchid Show—Annual orchid show sponsored by the local orchid society. March.

East-West International Fair—Cultural exhibits, performances, music, and food at the East-West Cultural Center.

THE GODS OF HAWAII

Of the thousands of gods worshipped by the ancient Hawaiians, only four—Kane, Ku, Kanaloa, and Lono—were believed to hold power.

Kane was worshipped as the creator of life. According to legend, Kane created the three worlds: the upper heavens where the gods lived, the lower heavens just above the earth, and earth itself.

In the old stories, Kane appears often with Kanaloa, about whom there are few details although some stories seem to equate Kanaloa with the devil of the Christian faith. In those tales, Kanaloa is banished to the underworld for rebelling against Kane.

Ku and his wife Hina were the symbols of all ancestors, past and future. The Hawaiians worshipped Ku to seek success in fishing, hunting, farming, and raising a large family. Ku, through a number of transformations, was also the god of war. He appeared in that role under the names Kukailimoku (Snatcher of Land) and Kuwahailo (Ku of the Mouthful of Maggots). These were fierce and blood-thirsty gods, and the temples (heiaus) were built so humans could be sacrificed to please Ku's altar egos (pardon the pun).

Lono, the god of weather and agriculture, was far more benign, and the only sacrifice to him was an offering of food, fruit or vegetable, left in the doorway of the house.

Buddha Day—A pageant of flowers with parades and other activities. April.

Lei Day—Celebration of the flower lei with music, hula, food, and sales of fantastic leis. May 1.

Royal Mausoleum Lei Decorating—Leis are placed on the graves of Hawaii's royal family. May.

Pacific Handcrafters Guild Spring Fair—The best artisans of the island display and sell their creations at this festival. May.

King Kamehameha Day—Parades, fairs, and other activ-

Those are the four major gods. A fifth god, a lesser deity, is more popular today than centuries ago. Madame Pele, the goddess of volcanoes, was said to have been a human who traveled to Oahu and became famous as a powerful sorceress. Pele was killed in a lava explosion, the legend goes, but her spirit returned and is said to live now in the Kilauea Crater on the Big Island.

Her anger has been attributed to several recent eruptions. One story says that when developers wanted to build in the Warm Springs area on the Big Island's south shore, they were warned by islanders that Pele would act to prevent the project. The developers scoffed, but before the project could get underway in 1955, a huge eruption lasting 88 days buried the Warm Springs area under lava.

A scientist friend of ours has studied Hawaii's volcanoes for years, and insists she has never seen Madame Pele. But other scientists and workers studying the volcanoes, she concedes, have reported seeing the spirit of Pele.

Rangers at the Volcanoes National Park tell other stories of visitors returning volcanic rocks taken from the island because Pele had punished them with bad luck for removing the black stones. Another folk tale? Perhaps. And perhaps it was just a coincidence that our two sons—Clayton and Jonathan—took volcanic stones from the Big Island in 1990 and, two months later, each suffered a fractured left foot while playing in separate football games on the same day.

---

ities honor the king who united the islands. June.

International Festival of the Pacific—Concerts, dance, and food celebrating the cultures of the Polynesian and Pacific Rim nations. July.

Prince Lot Hula Festival—A festival honoring King Kamehameha V, with ancient and modern hula dances, music, and more in the Moanaloa Gardens. July.

Bon Odori Season—Buddhist festival that honors ancestors with music and dance. Late July/August.

Floating Lantern Ceremony—Paper lanterns bearing the names of the dead float from the Waikiki-Kapahula Public Library on the canal to the McCully Bridge. The Buddhist ceremony celebrates the return of the spirits to a pure land. August.

Okinawan Festival—Parades, dances, arts, crafts, and more mark this celebration by this island ethnic group. September.

Aloha Week—A celebration of Hawaii's culture, with music, dance, parades, crafts, food, and more. September/October.

Wailea Ho'olaule—Two-day festival marking Hawaiian heritage. October.

Hawaiian Craftsmen Annual Juried Show—The best of island arts at the Amfac Gallery in Honolulu. October.

Academy Folk Art Bazaar—Craft show and sale at the Nolulu Academy of Arts. November.

Triple Crown of Surfing—Surfing the Banzai Pipeline on the north shore beaches. December.

For more information about the festivals and the exact dates, contact the visitors information offices listed earlier.

Where to Stay

Choosing the right hotel and resort for you is not merely a matter of money. What's romantic and interesting for you may not be so for someone else. Some resorts are big and busy, with lots of organized activities. And some hotels and inns are small and low-key, preferring to leave their guests alone to enjoy the resort on their own. We feel that the resorts, hotels, and inns listed here are special places. The price breakdown we have is as follows:

Expensive—$200 or more a night for a standard double room
Moderate—$100 to $200 a night for a standard double room
Inexpensive—Less than $100 a night for a standard double room.

At some resorts, meal plans are available that may save you money. The drawback is that the Map (Modified American Plan) restricts your flexibility in trying restaurants elsewhere.

Our Favorite Hotels and Resorts in Waikiki:

Aston Waikikian on the Beach—Gardens, thatched roofs, Polynesian architecture and decor make this hotel on the Duke Kahanamoku Lagoon a special place. Facilities include 135 nicely furnished rooms, which open to the gardens, a pool, and the sand beach on the lagoon. Moderate. 1811 Ala Moana Blvd., Honolulu, HI 96815. 808/949-5331 or 800/367-5124.

Diamond Head Beach Hotel—Quiet and small, this 53-unit hotel offers fine accommodations and a serene oceanfront location on the east end of the Waikiki shore. Moderate. 2947 Kalakaua Ave., Honolulu, HI 96815. 808/922-1928 or 800/367-6046.

Colony Surf—This small, luxury hotel offers apartments, not rooms. The hotel is located in the Diamond Head end of Waikiki, a much quieter location for those who like the view but appreciate the silence. Each of the 50 beautiful rooms have a full kitchen and sitting area. The hotel has a long reputation for first-class service and attention to its guests' needs. Another 50 units are available in the Colony Surf East next door, but the rooms are smaller. Expensive. 2895 Kalakaua Ave., Honolulu, HI 96815. 808/923-5751 or 800/367-6046.

Halekulani Hotel—Built around the stately Halekulani Hotel that dates back to 1931, this modern luxury hotel is the finest in Waikiki. The 456 rooms are large and tastefully decorated in woods and marble, and all have lanais and sitting areas. Ask for an ocean view. Outside attractions include a pool, famous for the orchid mosaic formed by its tiles, and a nice beach. Expensive. 2199 Kalia Rd., Honolulu, HI 96815. 808/923-2311 or 800/367-2343.

Hilton Hawaiian Village—The largest resort in the state, this massive complex of 2,524 rooms was recently renovated and landscaped. The result is a resort that looks new and offers everything a visitor needs: beautiful, spacious rooms in four towers overlooking the beach; five restaurants; one, two-level superpool and two normal pools; waterfalls; fish ponds; gardens; and water sports. The rooms are attractively decorated in bamboo and tropical colors. The only things missing are tennis and golf. But, of course, even that can be arranged. Expensive. 2005 Kalia Rd., Honolulu, HI 96815. 808/949–4321 or 800/HILTONS.

Hyatt Regency Waikiki—It's typical Hyatt: twin ten-story towers flank the fantastic atrium, two-story waterfalls, huge works of art, shops, and a constant whirl of activity in the lobby. The 1,234 rooms are spacious and comfortable. The hotel is across the street from the beach. Facilities include a pool and more than 70 shops. Moderate. 2424 Kalakaua Ave., Honolulu, HI 06815. 808/922–9292 or 800/228–9000.

Royal Hawaiian Hotel—Perhaps the most beautiful on Oahu, the Pink Palace was built in 1927 and has remained a gracious hotel with fine furniture, an air of old-style elegance and first-class service. There are 527 rooms in this stately mansion, but stick to the rooms in the original hotel, not the newer addition. After all, by staying in the new tower, you would miss the point. Facilities include gardens and a pool. Expensive. 2259 Kalakaua Ave., Honolulu, HI 96815. 808/923–7311 or 800/325–3535.

Waikiki Parc—This off-beach hotel offers 298 rooms ranging from inexpensive all the way up to rooms with rates to match the highest bracket on the strip. Save some bucks and book the least expensive. The rooms are comfortable, and many have sitting areas. Decor includes rattan furniture and pastel colors. Facilities include a pool and recreation deck. Inexpensive and up. 22–33 Helumoa Rd., Honolulu, HI 96815. 808/921–7272 or 800/422–0450.

Our Choices Elsewhere on the Island:

Kahala Hilton—Perhaps the finest resort on the island, this secluded retreat on the east side of Diamond Head is elegant and low-key. A favorite with dignitaries and movie stars, the hotel has 310 rooms and suites and 84 cottage units. All the rooms are huge and furnished with the taste and style one would expect in such an elegant resort. The service is first-class. Facilities include a pool, tennis courts, lagoon with dolphins and other sea life, and a fitness center nearby but off the premises. Expensive. 5000 Kahala Ave., Honolulu, HI 96816. 808/734–2211 or 800/ 367–2525.

Manoa Valley Inn—This intimate, 70-year-old hotel in the Manoa Valley offers seven rooms and a cottage furnished with antiques, four-poster beds, and other nice touches. Only the cottage and four of the rooms have private baths. Moderate. 2001 Vancouver Dr., Honolulu, HI 96822. 808/947–6019 or 800/634–5115.

Sheraton Makaha Resort and Country Club—This Polynesian-style resort offers lovely rooms furnished with island woods and colorful fabrics. The setting is also glorious: the verdant Makaha Valley on Oahu's leeward shore. Facilities include golf, tennis, stables, and pool. Expensive. P.O. Box 8906, Makaha, HI 06792. 808/695–9511 or 800/334–8484.

Turtle Bay Hilton—This is the largest of the few resorts on Oahu's windward north shore. The 437 rooms and cottages are spacious and nicely furnished with brass, wicker, and pastel fabrics. All the rooms have lanais. The small but comfortable cottages are perfect for a romantic getaway. Facilities include pool, golf, tennis, stables, and a beach. Expensive. P.O. Box 187, Kahuku, HI 96731. 808/293–8811 or 800/HILTONS.

For smaller inns and bed and breakfasts, contact Bed and Breakfast Hawaii at P.O. Box 449, Kapaa, HI 96746, 808/822–7771 or 800/367–8047, ext. 339; Bed & Breakfast Honolulu, 3242 Kaohinani Dr., Honolulu, HI 96817, 808/595–7533 or 800/ 367–8047, ext. 351; and Pacific Hawaii Bed & Breakfast, 19 Kai Nani Pl., Kailua, HI 96743. 808/262–6026.

Where to Dine

The better restaurants on the islands are usually in the finest resorts. However, for those willing to venture outside their resort or hotel, some special dining rooms await. Always make reservations and always ask about the dress code.

The price categories for restaurants, for two persons for dinner, excluding wine, tips, and taxes, are:

Expensive—More than $75.
Moderate—$25 to $75.
Inexpensive—Less than $25.

Our choices in Waikiki:

Baci—The location, a busy shopping/office center, isn't the best, but this Italian dining room in the Waikiki Trade Center serves exceptional northern Italian nouvelle cuisine. The best are the fresh fish and pasta dishes and the Frutti di Mare seafood stew. Moderate. 2255 Kuhio Ave., 808/924–2533.

Bon Appetit—This elegant pink-and-black bistro decorated with art and collectibles from France serves country French dishes in an intimate environment. The salmon, trout, and lobster dishes are your best choices. Moderate. 1779 Ala Moana Blvd. 808/942–3837.

Colony Surf—If you are seeking a beautiful room loaded with romantic touches—crystal, music, candlelight, mirrors—come to Michel's in this hotel. The cuisine is continental, and the steak and seafood are superb. Expensive. 2895 Kalakaua Ave. 808/923–6552.

Five Spice—The menu is huge at this small dining room, and the dishes offered range from Szechuan to Cantonese to Mandarin to vegetarian. The pork and shrimp dishes are superb, and the vegetarian offerings are interesting enough to make you consider swearing off meat. Inexpensive. 432 Ena Rd. 808/955–8706.

Halekulani Hotel—The finest dining room at this fantastic hotel is La Mer, where French and Hawaiian cuisine are blended to create an often sensational sensory experience. The complete dinner menus are good bets here, where everything is excellent and beautifully presented. Expensive. 2199 Kalaia Rd. 808/923–2311.

Hau Tree Lanai—This beachfront restaurant offers superb brunch fare: omelets, waffles, and the like. The location is very romantic. Inexpensive. New Otani Kaimana Beach Hotel, 2863 Kalakaua Ave. 808/923–1555.

Hilton Hawaiian Village—There are two restaurants of note at this resort. Bali by the Sea, the oceanside room, is a continental restaurant that is famous for its duck and fish dishes. It's expensive. The Golden Dragon, favored by many local Chinese, serves Szechuan and Cantonese dishes. The favorites include stir-fried lobster and Peking duck. Moderate. 2005 Kalia Rd. 808/949–4321.

Hyatt Regency Waikiki—The best of the dining rooms at this hotel is Bagwells 2424, where the decor—antiques, waterfall, etched glass, oriental artworks—can overwhelm you at this beautiful restaurant. Nouvelle Hawaiian dishes are the star attractions, with the seafood dishes the most consistent winners. Your best bet may be the grazing menu, which will allow you to try a small serving of a dish for one-fourth the price. Expensive. 2424 Kalakaua Ave. 808/922–9292.

Nick's Fishmarket—Seafood is the attraction at this restaurant/dinner club. All the seafood dishes are excellent, and dinner comes with music and dancing. Expensive. 2070 Kalakaua Ave. 808/955–6333.

Orchid—Imagine enjoying a sumptuous Sunday brunch at a lovely restaurant with grand views of Diamond Head. You can at Orchids, where in the midst of the blossoms you can munch on a brunch serving up excellent sashimi, curries, and the more familiar brunch dishes like eggs Benedict. Moderate. 2199 Kalia Rd. 808/923–2311.

Suntory—This elegant Japanese restaurant has a sushi bar, a shabu shabu room serving sliced beef in broth, a teppanyaki room where the food is cooked on a grill, and a private dining room. The ambience is a bit formal, but the creative seafood entrees are among the finest on the island. Moderate. 2233 Kalakaua Ave. 808/922–5511.

Our Choices Elsewhere on the Island:

Black Orchid—This formal art-deco-style restaurant is partially owned by movie and TV star Tom Selleck. Even without Selleck it would have a claim to fame for its fine cajun tuna, marinated prawns, and other seafood delights. Expensive. 500 Ala Moana Blvd., Honolulu. 808/521–3111.

Crouching Lion Inn—A beautiful setting overlooking the ocean makes this a special place. The food is simple fare, featuring steaks, homemade soups, and the like. Great spot for lunch. Moderate. 51–666 Kamehameha Highway in Kaaawa. 808/237–8511.

Haiku Gardens—Magnificent gardens, ponds, and foliage make this restaurant a romantic stop. The food features mesquite-broiled beef and ribs, but also try the Hawaiian dishes like the roast pig and chicken long rice. Moderate. 44–336 Haiku Rd. in Kaneohe. 808/247–6671.

Ideta Restaurant—Exceptional sushi served in an authentic Japanese-style sushi bar. Moderate. 620 Kohou St., Kalihi. 808/ 847–4844.

Kahala Hilton—The best resort on the island has one of the top dining rooms, too. Maile is beautiful, decorated with lava-rock walls, orchids, and waterfalls. The table d'hote menu usually features many fine fish dishes, but also consider the excellent roast rack of lamb, the duckling Waialae, or the opakapaka. Expensive. 5000 Kahala Ave., east of Diamond Head. 808/521–3111.

Ono Hawaiian Foods—Casual and inexpensive and perhaps the finest and most authentic Hawaiian food on the island. Try the kalua pig or the beef stews. Inexpensive. 726 Kapahulu Ave., Kapahulu. 808/737–2275.

Steamer's—The daily seafood specials are the best selections at this casual but good dining room in the Haleiwa Shopping Center on the north shore. Moderate. 66–165 Kamehameha Highway, in Haleiwa. 808/637–5071.

Sunset Grill—The decor may be casual but there is nothing lax about the broiled seafood at this fine dining room. Moderate. 500 Ala Moana Blvd., Honolulu. 808/521–4409.

The Willows—The setting is lovely. The grass-roof dining pavilions are surrounded by gardens and carp-filled ponds. The cuisine is a bit of everything, from sauteed opakapaka with spinach to curried salads and meat dishes. All are excellent. For a real Hawaiian feast, try the Kamaaina luncheon on Thursdays. Reservations are required for the luncheon, which usually includes a hula and music show. Moderate. 901 Hausten St., Honolulu. 808/946–4808.

Luaus and Other Nightlife

More so than any other island, Oahu offers more in nightlife and cultural activities that any visitor could ever experience. We have organized the activities into the following categories:

Luaus

The most authentic luau on the island is the Hanohano Family Luau, a day-long experience in which you help prepare the luau feast, play games, go fishing, and enjoy many other activities. Transportation to the luau in Punaluu on the north shore is provided from most hotels. The cost is about $40 for adults. Call 808/949–5559.

Other popular luaus are the Paradise Cove Luau on the eastern shore (daily at 5:00 PM, 808/973–5828); the Royal Luau in the Royal Hawaiian Hotel (Monday at 6:00 PM, 808/923–7311); and Germaine's Luau, a huge event that draws about a thousand from the Waikiki strip (daily at 6:00 PM, 808/941–3338). The cost usually starts at about $30–$35 per person, and includes the luau and transportation from many Waikiki hotels. Check with your hotel tour desk.

Hotel Nightclubs

Call first about show times, cover charges, and other costs.

Al Harrington—Harrington and his cast of 16 dancers and

musicians put on a very entertaining show. Two shows nightly. Polynesian Palace, Reef Towers Hotel, 247 Lewers St. 808/ 923-9861.

Don Ho—"The Entertainer" of the islands stars at his Vegas-style Polynesian revue in the Dome at the Hilton Hawaiian Village every night but Saturday. 2005 Kalia Rd. 808/949-4321.

Kahala Hilton—Danny Kaleikini and his songs and stories have been the mainstay at this elegant resort for more than two decades. Shows Monday-Saturday. 5000 Kahala Ave. 808/734-2211.

Monarch's—This club in the Royal Hawaiian is popular for its tea dances on Sunday from 4:30 PM to 8:00 PM, and for the Brothers Cazimero and their Hawaiian dinner show, Tuesday–Thursday. 2257 Kalakaua Ave. 808/923-7311.

Nick's Fishmarket—Intimate atmosphere and an upscale crowd make this dance room and restaurant a popular gathering spot. In the Waikiki Gateway Hotel, 2070 Kalakaua Ave. 808/ 955-6333.

Paradise Lounge—Dancing nightly to a pianist and a solo singer. Expensive, and it draws a well-heeled crowd. In the Hilton Hawaiian Village, 2005 Kalia Rd. 808/949-4321.

Society of Seven—For more than two decades, this lively group has been entertaining tourists and islanders with their contemporary music. Two shows every night but Wednesday, when there's one, and Sunday, when the room is dark. Outrigger Waikiki Hotel, 2335 Kalakaua Ave. 808/922-6408.

Dinner Shows and Nightspots

Call first about show times, cover charges, and other costs.

Black Orchid—Chic art-deco style restaurant offers live jazz. 500 Ala Moana Blvd. 808/521-3111.

Hawaiian Hoe-Down Country Barbecue—Call it a Western Luau, with cowboys dancing the hula, yodelers, the Cotton-Eye Joe, two-step dancing, and dinner. Heeia Park in Kaneohe. Shows Tuesday and Thursday, transportation provided. 808/922-3377.

Pecos River Cafe—Hawaii's top country and western cafe, this spot in the small town of Aiea is a place to go for casual fun. 99–016 Kamehameha Highway. 808/487–7980.

Polynesian Cultural Center—A colorful and entertaining show at the Mormon-sponsored center in Laie on the windward shore. Two shows nightly. 55–370 Kamehameha Highway, Laie. 808/293–3333.

Sea Life Hawaiian Revue—Sea Life not only does fish, they do Hawaiiana. The show is at 8:30 PM Thursday and Sunday and is performed at the Gallery, the casual restaurant at the park. The show—but not dinner or transportation—is included in the park admission fee ($8.50). Makapuu Point. 808/259–7933.

Dinner Cruises

The ships appear every evening before sunset off the Waikiki shore. From the beach, they look elegant and inviting, but these dinner cruises are often crowded and disappointing, with mediocre food and unexciting entertainment. If you must sail off into the sunset for a dinner and show, try Tradewind Charters (808/533–0220), which offers a sailing experience limited to six passengers. Other options (but don't say we didn't warn you) are Hawaiian Cruises' Sunset Dinner Sail (550 passengers, Polynesian revue) at 808/947–9971; Alii Kai Catamarans (1,000 passengers, dancing and show) at 808/524–1800; and the Windjammer Cruises (1,500 passengers, Polynesian revue) at 808/521–0036.

Music and Theater

American Theater Company Hawaii—Features some name actors and island professionals starring in a number of different plays each season. Call 808/599–5122.

Chamber Music Hawaii—Holds 25 concerts a year. Call 808/531–6617 for the schedule and location.

Hawaii Opera Theater—Has a two-month season (February and March), with performances in the Neal Blaisdell Concert Hall, Ward Avenue and King streets. Call 808/537–6191.

Honolulu Community Theater—Presents musicals and dramas each year. Call 808/734–0274.

The Honolulu Symphony—Has its season from September to April, with concerts at the Neal Blaisdell Concert Hall. Call 808/942-2200.

Kumu Kahua—This island troupe offers five plays a season about life in Hawaii. The shows are in the Tenney Theatre on the grounds of St. Andrew's Cathedral, 224 St. Emma's Square. Call 808/599-1503.

Horseback riding is a popular diversion in the islands.
(Photo courtesy of Patti Cook & Associates)

CHAPTER 7

Island Adventures

*B*eyond the beaches, away from the fabulous resorts, is a Hawaii filled with adventure. On these islands you can soar over volcanoes, explore rain forests thick with mists and mysteries, dive along a reef filled with exotic fish, take a boat out to see the wintering humpback whales, and bicycle down dormant volcanoes.

For the more adventurous (and prosperous) you can even dine in a king's palace, spend a day working as a paniolo (cowboy) and be flown by helicopter to a jungle glade where you will enjoy a gourmet meal next to a waterfall.

The adventures we recommend may be arranged through your hotel's tour desk or concierge, or by calling the group directly.

Learning Vacations

Tired of just soaking up the rays on the beach? Try using your vacation time to learn something about Hawaii's exotic flora and fauna.

Questers Worldwide Nature Tours leads hikers into undeveloped wilderness areas to study plant and animal life. Contact them at 257 Park Ave. South, New York, NY 10010. 212/673–3120.

Oceanic Society Expeditions leads tours with an environmental theme, such as whale-watching, coral reef tours, and other sea adventures. Contact them at Fort Mason Center, Building E, San Francisco, CA 94123. 415/441–1106.

The Sierra Club offers camping trips with a conservation theme. Contact them at 730 Polk St., San Francisco, CA 94109. 415/776–2211.

The Smithsonian Institution's Associates Travel Program conducts tours exploring the natural beauty of the islands. Contact them at 1100 Jefferson Dr., SW, Washington, DC 20560. 202/357–4700.

The cost of these tours varies widely, but is usually a bit more than you would pay for a guided tour of similar length.

Fantasies

The Hyatt Regency Waikoloa on the Big Island has cornered the fantasy market. Their dream adventures include:

• A private dinner for up to four persons in the Hulihee Palace, the summer retreat of Hawaii's royalty. The five-course dinner is served by waiters in authentic Hawaiian attire. Entertainment suitable for a king is performed. The cost is $2,750.

• A private picnic at Lauhula Point, a 300-foot cliff overlooking magnificent waterfalls and valleys filled with mist and mystery. The point is accessible only by helicopter. For only about $1,400 two can fly to the point, have a gourmet picnic, and then take a one-hour tour of the Kohala Coast. Longer (and costlier) tours are available.

• Go swimming with a dolphin. The Hyatt's Dolphin Encounter is so popular that resort guests must enter a lottery for the chance to take part in the conservation-oriented program. No outsiders need apply. The cost is $65 for an adult.

• A sunset sail to a secluded beach for an intimate dinner for two. This package costs $1,470 and includes transportation by limousine to the boat and back.

• Spend a day on the Kahua Ranch living the life of a paniolo. This fantasy costs $2,150 for four persons and includes a tour of the ranch led by the ranch owner, as well as a guided day in the saddle riding and working the range.

Other fantasies include sunset sails, hunting expeditions on the Parker Ranch, hikes, scuba, and snorkeling trips.

Call American Express Travel Service at the Hyatt Regency Waikoloa. 808/885–1234, Ext. 51.

Airborne Tours

Hawaii's majestic scenery is often best appreciated from the air, where you can see the mountains and valleys too difficult to drive or walk into and where the lava flows are too fiery to get near.

On the Big Island, Kona Helicopters (808/329–1887), Mauna Kea Helicopters (808/885–6400), Volcano Heli-Tours (808/967–7578), Papillon Helicopters (808/883–8808), and Hawaii Pacific Aviation (808/961–5591) offer helicopter tours of the volcano park. IO Aviation (808/935–3031) provides tours by plane or helicopter.

On Kauai, the Na Pali Coast, the Waimea Canyon, and the lush jungle interior of Kauai are fantastic viewed from the air. Call ERA Helicopters (808/245–9555), or Menehune Helicopters (808/245–7705). Tradewinds Gliders has soaring trips. Call 808/245–6739.

Volcano and island sightseeing tours are offered by Maui Helicopters (808/879–1601), Papillon Hawaiian Helicopters (808/669–4884), Hawaii Helicopters (808/877–3900), and South Seas Helicopters (808/871–8844).

For those who prefer to be their own pilot, call Maui Soaring Supplies, which offers hang-gliding instruction, 808/878–1271.

On Molokai, Pacific Aviation International offers helicopter tours of the scenic north shore and its 2,000-foot cliffs and waterfalls. Call 808/567–6128 or 800/245–9696.

Hawaii Pacific Helicopters offers helicopter tours of Waikiki, the Pali Lookout, and other sights on Oahu. Call 808/836–1566.

The price varies, of course, depending on the length of the flight and the popularity of the flight chosen, but expect to pay from $100 to $300 per person.

Scuba Diving and Snorkeling

Hawaii's seas offer some fine reefs for diving and snorkeling, but the best places are not near the resorts. Scores of groups offer

CRUISING THE ISLANDS

Imagine yourself dancing on a moonlit deck surrounded by an ocean alive with starlight. In the distance, the shore is alive with lights, the tropical breezes gently sway the palm trees, and some unseen orchestra sends its notes out into the night.

This scene isn't entirely a fantasy. It can become a reality for travellers who choose to explore the Hawaiian islands on a cruise ship.

There are several cruise lines that stop in Hawaii, especially at Honolulu, on their way across the South Pacific, but only one—American Hawaii Cruises—offers a tour by ship around the islands.

American Hawaii Cruises operates two ships—the USS Constitution and the USS Independence—that make seven-day cruises out of Honolulu. The ports visited are Kahului on Maui, Hilo and Kailua-Kona on Hawaii, and Nawiliwili on Kauai. The ships cruise by Lanai and Molokai, but do not stop. The USS Constitution itinerary includes an overnight stop in Nawiliwili, while the USS Independence includes an overnight stop in Kahului.

The line also offers cruise/resort packages made up of

diving cruises to offshore reefs and sunken craters. For the best diving and snorkeling spots, ask at the following dive centers:

On Hawaii, try Dive Makai Charters (808/329–2025), Fair Wind Sail & Dive (808/322–2788), Jack's Diving Locker (800/345–4807 or 808/329–7585), Kona Coast Divers (808/329–8802), Nautilus Dive Center (808/935–3299).

On Kauai, diving trips can be arranged through Aquatics Kauai (800/822–9422 or 808/822–9213), Dive Kauai (808/822–0452), Fathom Five Divers (808/742–6991), Destination Hawaii (808/922–0975), and Sea Sage Diving Center (808/822–3841).

three- and four-day cruises with three- and four-night stays at selected resorts.

The cost of the seven-day cruise package is from about $1,000 to $3,900 per person, based on double occupancy. That fare includes all meals and entertainment, but not wine and other alcoholic drinks, tips, land-tour packages, or air fare. Air packages are available that can cut the cost of air fares by as much as 50 percent from many major U.S. airports.

The cost of the cruise/resort package ranges from $730 to $1,650 per person based on double occupancy. This includes all meals and entertainment on the cruise, the room at the resort (but not meals or entertainment at the resort), and air and land connections to the resort. Air fare from the mainland is not included.

The two ships can carry 798 passengers each, and each has two pools, a fitness center, Hawaiian cultural programs, nightly entertainment, and tour desks at which you can arrange rental cars and land tours.

For more information, contact American Hawaii Cruises, 550 Kearney St., San Francisco, CA 94108 or call 800/227–3666.

On Maui, the best diving spots are on the southwest shore. Contact Lahaina Divers (808/667–7496), Captain Nemo's Ocean Emporium (808/661–5555), Dive Maui (808/667–2080), Central Pacific Divers (800/551–6767 or 808/661–8718), Extended Horizons (808/661–0611), or Hawaiian Reef Divers (808/667–7647).

On Oahu, try Dan's Dive Shop (808/536–6181), Destination Hawaii (808/922–0975), Steve's Diving Adventures (808/947–8900), and the Aloha Dive Shop (808/395–5922).

Only certified divers are taken on the dives. Most of these tour operators offer lessons. The cost ranges from about $60 per person and up, depending on the length of the trip and the size of the group taken. Most operators offer weekly dive packages.

On Molokai, there are no group-led snorkeling or diving expeditions, but you can rent equipment at the Molokai Fish and Dive (808/553–3392).

A popular place for snorkeling off Maui is the Molokini Crater, a mostly submerged extinct volcano whose sunken basin serves as a haven for fish and divers. It can get crowded. Call the Ocean Activities Center (808/879–4485), Wave (808/667–6233), Four Winds (808/879–9994), Sail Hawaii (808/879–2201), and Trilogy Excursions (808/661–4743).

Snorkeling trips on Kauai are offered by Blue Water Sailing (808/822–0525), Hawaiian Z-Boat Company (808/826–9274), and Captain Andy's Sailing Adventure (808/822–7833).

For snorkeling on Hawaii, contact Captain Zodiac Raft Expedition (808/329–3199) and Captain Cook VII (808/329–6411).

For snorkeling on Oahu, call South Seas Aquatics (808/735–0437) or Waikiki Diving (808/922–7188).

Snorkeling rates usually start at about $35 per person and go up according to the length of the trip.

Surfing

Surfing conditions in the islands are nearly perfect, for the lack of a continental shelf around the islands means the waves of the north Pacific are not slowed before they curl and rush toward the shore.

On Oahu, Waikiki Beach Services at the Outrigger Hotel (808/923–1111) and the Sheraton Waikiki offer lessons and board rentals. The Haleiwa Surf Center at the Alii Beach Park on Oahu's north shore is where the big rollers come in. Surfing lessons are offered for free on weekends. Call 808/637–5051.

On Hawaii, you can rent boards at Orchid Land Surfboards in Hilo (808/935–1533) and Pacific Vibrations in Kailua-Kona (808/329–4140). The best surfing beaches are on the south shore.

On Maui, Honolua Bay and Hookpia Beach Park are popular with surfers. Boards can be rented at the Lahaina Beach Center in Lahaina (808/661–5762).

On Kauai, the best surfing is on the north shore, particularly Hanalei Bay. Boards can be rented from Pedal & Paddle in Hanalei (808/826–9069) and at Progressive Expressions in Koloa (808/742–6041).

Board rentals range from $10 to $20 a day, and lessons start at about $15 for a one-hour group class.

Windsurfing

Hawaii's waters are made for all levels of windsurfers: quiet coves for the beginner and windswept bays for the expert.

On Oahu, call Aloha Windsurfing (808/926–1185) or Windsurfing Hawaii's Kailua Beach School (808/261–3539), which offers hotel pickups.

On Hawaii, call Captain Nemo's Ocean Sports in Waikoloa (808/885–5555).

On Maui, call the Magic Maui Windsurfing Center in Kahului (808/877–4816).

On Kauai, try Hanalei Sailboards in Hanalei (808/826–9732) or Waiohai Beach Services in Poipu (808/742–9511).

Lessons start from $30 for a two-hour introductory class; rentals range from $10 per hour, with lower rates for half-day and full-day rentals.

Fishing

Hawaii's deep blue waters are a prime fishing ground. Charter boats catch blue marlin, mahimahi, wahoo, tuna, and many other sport fish.

On Hawaii, deep sea fishing charters are offered by Happy Time Fishing Charters (800/367–8014), Aerial Sportfishing Kona (808/329–5603), the Kona Activities Center (808/329–3171), and A-1 Black Bart Sportfishing (800/367–8047, ext. 432 or 808/ 329–3000).

On Kauai, call Alana Lynn Too Charters (808/245–7446), Gent-Lee Fishing (808/245–7504), and Seascape Kauai (808/ 826–1111). Freshwater fishing is also popular on the Garden Isles. For bass, call Cast & Catch Freshwater Bass Guides (808/ 332–9707) and Bass Guides of Kauai (808/822–1405).

On Maui, call Excel Charters (808/877–3333), Classic Activity Connections (808/661–5344), and Aloha Activity Center (808/222–4856).

On Molokai, the Alele II Charters offers deep sea fishing trips (808/558–8266).

And while on Oahu, contact Coreene-C Charters (808/536–7472), Inter-Island Sportfishing Ltd. (808/533–3330), and Island Charters (808/536–1555).

Prices start at about $300 per person for a full day; $200 for a half-day charter.

Bicycling

With the exceptions of Honolulu and the steep mountain roads, Hawaii's highways are perfect for bicycling. They are often flat, or nearly so, lightly traveled, and well maintained.

Several groups offer bicycling tours of the Big Island. Backroads Bicycle Touring offers 10-day, 200-mile tours of the Big Island. Packages usually include hotels and meals. Bicycles, airfare, and other charges are extra. Contact them at 415/527–4005. Hawaiian Eyes has two- to six-hour tours (808/885–8806), Island Bicycle Adventures has five-night guided tours (808/955–6789), and On the Loose Bicycle Vacations has 7- and 10-day trips (415/ 527–4005 or 800/346–6712).

On Kauai, North Shore Bike, Cruise and Snorkel offers a full-day guided biking trip on the rural north shore, with a barbecue lunch at the Bali Hai beach (808/822–1582).

One of the more unusual adventures on Maui is to take a bicycle ride from the top of Haleakala down the slope of the volcano. Maui Mountain Cruisers (808/232-MAUI), Maui Downhill (808/871–2155), and Cruiser Bob's Original Haleakala Downhill (808/654–7717) all offer transportation to the summit, meals, a bike, training, and safety gear.

The costs range from a minimal fee for bike rental to more than $600 for a multiday trip in which lodging, meals, and equipment are included.

Stargazing

The summit of Mauna Kea on Hawaii is said to be the finest location in the world for stargazing. Numerous observatories are located on the summit (13,796 feet), where the Onizuka Center for International Astronomy is located. Free tours are offered at 2:00 PM and 6:30 PM Saturday and at 2:00 PM Sunday. Reservations may be required; call 808/935–3371.

The tours are free, but you must provide your own transportation. You will need a four-wheel-drive vehicle to reach the summit.

Hunting

It was a surprise to us, but Hawaii is also a popular destination with hunters. Pheasant, sheep, axis deer, and wild boar are found on many of the islands. Most of the hunts are guided and are conducted by the larger ranches on the islands.

On Hawaii, contact Hawaii Hunting Tours (808/776–1666), Ginger Flower Enterprises (808/324–1444), or the McCandless Ranch (808/328–2389).

On Lanai, guided hunts are available through the Koele Company (808/531–4454). The main game are axis deer, wild turkey, and partridge.

Hunting Adventures of Maui offers guided hunts on a private ranch. Game includes wild boar and mountain goats. Call 808/572–8214. The Hana Ranch has boar and pheasant hunts. Call 808/248–7238.

Axis deer and numerous fowl are hunted on Molokai. Contact the Molokai Ranch (808/552–2767), which offers guided hunts.

Licenses are needed and are issued from November through the third weekend of January. Contact the State Department of Land and Natural Resources (808/961–3707).

The costs vary widely, depending on whether you want a single hunt or a more elaborate package that includes meals and lodging. Contact the outfitter for more details.

Wildlife Safari

See unusual African and Asian animals as well as the islands' own axis deer at the Molokai Ranch Wildlife Safari. Tours of the 1,000-acre refuge are offered by van from the Kaluakoi Hotel and Golf Club. Call 808/552–2555. The tours cost about $12. There are four tours daily.

Tours on Horseback

The vast open spaces found on many of the islands are perfect for horseback riding. The outfitters listed here conduct guided rides on forest trails or on the vast expanse of rangelands that resemble scenes from an Old West movie.

Many of the larger resorts have their own stables. If you are not staying at those on the Big Island, contact Ironwood Outfitters (808/885–4941), Waikoloa Countryside Stables (808/883–9335), Waiono Meadow Trails Ride (808/324–1544), and Waipio on Horseback (808/885–7484).

On Kauai, guided rides are offered by CJM Country Stables (808/245–6666) and Pooku Stables (808/826–6777). Three-hour cowboy breakfast rides are also offered by CJM Stables.

On Maui, guided rides are offered by Adventures on Horseback (808/242–7445); Aloha Nui Loa Tours (808/669–0000); Hotel Hana-Maui Stables (808/248–8284), which has rides on a working cattle ranch; Kaanapali Kau Lio (808/667–7896); Makena Stables (808/879–0244), which offers rides on a 30,000-acre ranch on the south shore; Charley's Trail Rides & Pack Trips (808/248–8209); Pony Express Tours (808/667–2200); and at the Rainbow Ranch (808/669–4991).

On Molokai, Horse Heaven is your only choice (808/552–0056). The rides offered are five hours long and take place on the Kalaupapa cliffs.

Oahu has some wonderful countryside for riding. Try the Kualoa Ranch (808/237–8515), Sheraton Makaha Lio Stables (808/695–9511) and the Turtle Bay Hilton (808/293–8811).

Costs vary widely. Call the stables and ask about hourly and daily rates.

Mule Rides

On the Molokai northern coast, Rare Adventures offers a seven-hour mule ride from the Kalae Stables down to the leper colony at Kalaupapa. The mule ride is safe, though a bit exciting, and there is no health danger from visiting the colony. The Rare Adventures tour includes the mule ride, a tour of the colony, and lunch. The cost is about $75 per person. Call 808/552–2622 or 800/843–5978.

Skiing Mauna Kea

The summit of Mauna Kea gets snow almost every winter, but skiing there is for advanced skiers only. Two groups offer ski trips: Ski Guides Hawaii (808/885–4188) and Ski Shop Hawaii (808/737–4394).

The View From the Top

The summit of Mauna Kea is the best place to see the world around you. If you want to go to the top, call Paradise Safaris (808/322–2366), Hawaii Resorts Transportation Company (808/885–7484), and the Waipio Valley Shuttle (808/775–7121).

THE FOODS OF HAWAII

The cuisine of Hawaii is as diverse as its peoples and reflects the many cultures and backgrounds of the native Hawaiians as well as the many Asian immigrants.

While the menus in most of the more expensive restaurants will seem familiar—fresh local fish, huge shrimp, roast duckling, veal scallopini, lobster, steak, and prime rib—the influence of the Pacific Rim nations and the island culture can be seen in the appetizers and some of the more unusual entrees.

Sashimi (thinly sliced raw fish usually served with a hot sauce), particularly charred sashimi, is often offered as both an appetizer and entree. Sushi (raw fish and rice), tempura (lightly battered and fried fish and vegetables), dim sum (steamed or fried pastries stuffed with vegetable or meat fillings), and other Asian dishes are also common.

Saimin, a noodle served in a chicken or fish soup, is so popular on the islands that it is even found on the menus at McDonald's restaurants.

Many island foods and cooking methods had their beginnings with the luau. They include: lomilomi salmon (salmon shredded and mixed with chopped green onions, tomatoes, and crushed ice); poi (a pastelike substance made from mashed taro, a sweet potato-like vegetable); haupia (coconut pudding); and lau laus (taro tops, cooked with coconut milk, chicken, and seafood). Curried dishes are also popular.

Also prized by islanders is the traditional whole pig roasted in an imu, which is a large, shallow hole in the ground lined with

Submarine Rides

We took our first ride on a sightseeing submarine in the Caribbean. These 40-passenger ships dive as deep as 100 feet and take you along the beautiful reefs accessible only to fish and scuba divers. What we saw through the large viewing port-

lava rocks. A wood fire is built in the hole. When the rocks are thoroughly heated, the fire and ashes are removed, and ti or banana leaves are then placed in the pit. The pig or other main course (and sometimes the side dishes) are placed in the pit and covered with more leaves and finally a thick cover made of woven banana leaves. The leaves inside the pit give off steam, which, along with the heat from the stones, cooks the meal.

Beef is popular in the islands, particularly on Hawaii and Maui, where some of the largest cattle ranches in the world are found.

Aquaculture—the cultivation of fish—has been practiced for centuries on the islands. Ancient fish ponds remain in use near Nawiliwili Bay on Kauai and on other islands. Modern aquacultural projects raise trout and salmon on the islands.

The local ocean fish are popular with diners. Some fish commonly found on island menus are familiar to mainland visitors, but not by their island names. Here are some of the more common fish served: 'ahi (yellowfin tuna), mahimahi (dolphin fish), ono (wahoo), uku (gray snapper), kaku (barracuda), 'ula 'ula (red snapper), 'ama'ama (mullet), kamanu (Hawaiian salmon) 'opakapaka (pink snapper), and puhi (eel).

Island game animals are not overlooked by local chefs. Axis deer is found on many menus, either served as medallions or even in sausage, as we found in the Lodge at Koele's magnificent dining room on the island of Lanai.

Other foods that are especially good and flavorful on the islands include the strong Kona coffee, fresh pineapples, liliko'o (passionfruit), and macadamia nuts.

holes was an amazing world of color unlike anything we have seen while snorkeling.

There are two Atlantis submarines operating in Hawaii. The Atlantis IV makes dives along coral reefs on the Big Island's Kona Coast. The submarine operates out of the wharf at Kailua-Kona.

Call 808/329–6626. On Oahu, the Atlantis submarine sails out of Port Hilton at the Hilton Hawaiian Village, 2005 Kalia Rd. Call 808/536–2694.

The cost is about $60 per adult.

Coastal Cruises

Zodiacs are small, rubberized boats that are safe and speedy and offer exciting rides along the shore. On Hawaii, Captain Zodiac (808/329–3199) offers tours of the western coast and rafting expeditions.

On Kauai, two groups offer sea tours of the Na Pali Coast and other shores of Kauai. Captain Zodiac is the best known (808/826–9371), but Na Pali-Kauai Boat Charters (800/367–8047 or 808/826–7254) is also popular.

The Na Pali Queen, a 130-foot luxury ship, offers a trip along the Na Pali Coast, a barbecue, snorkeling, and a zodiac ride to a deserted beach. Call 808/246–1015.

On Molokai, Whistling Swan Charters offers three-day trips of the north shore. Call 808/553–5238.

Four-Wheel-Drive Tours

Hawaii Hunting Tours offers four-wheel-drive tours of the Parker Ranch, Mauna Kea and Mauna Loa, the Waipio Valley, and other regions of the Big Island. These are not hunting expeditions. Lunch is included. Call 808/776–1666.

Adventures 4-Wheel Drive Kauai offers tours of the Polihale Beach area and the scenic seafront cliffs there (808/245–9622), and Kauai Mountain Tours has all-day journeys to the Na Pali-Kona Forest Preserve and the east side of the Waimea Canyon. Call 808/245–7224.

On Lanai, Off-Road Tours offers two-hour tours for up to three people of the major attractions on this tiny island. Call 808/565–6952.

Hunting Adventures of Maui offers off-road sightseeing and

photo safaris on private ranches. Call 808/572–8214 or 808/977–8921.

The cost of these tours starts at about $75 per person and goes up, depending on the length of the trip and its difficulty.

Hiking Tours

To really see the beauty of Hawaii, you must get out of your car and walk into the forests filled with orchids, exotic plants, and strange trees. Four groups offer to help you, with regularly scheduled hiking tours of the major natural attractions. Hawaiian Walkways offers half-day and up to three-day treks; call 808/325–6777. Other outfitters are Pacific Quest (808/638–8338), Trek Hawaii (808/523–1302), and Wilderness Hawaii (808/737–4697).

Hike Maui (808/879–5270) offers 50 different hikes led by owner/naturalist Ken Schmitt and Outer Island Adventures (808/572–6396) has a number of one-day walks.

On Molokai, Rare Adventures (808/552–2622 or 800/843–5978) offers hikes into the Kalaupapa.

On Oahu, you can guide yourself and climb Diamond Head (808/923–1555) or join the Hawaii Trail & Mountain Club, which holds hikes on Sundays (808/734–5515).

The costs range from free or a minimal fee for the club walks and goes up to more than $50 per person.

Whale-Watching Cruise

Each winter, the majestic humpback whales spend the season feeding off the islands' coasts. It's an incredible sight; one you should not miss. A number of organizations have trips to see the whales. Call Pacific Whale Foundation (808/879–8811 or 800/WHALE–1–1). On Maui, call Ocean Activities Center (808/879–4484), Alihilani Charters (808/871–1156), Seabird Excursions (808/661–3643), Leilani Cruises (808/661–8397), and Trilogy Excursions (808/661–4743).

Tickets start at about $35 per person.

Historical Tours

Hawaii Resorts Transportation has a guided tour that looks at the historical spots on the Kona Coast. Call 808/885–7484.

Damien Molokai Tours leads very interesting, four-hour tours of what once was a leper's colony on Molokai. Call 808/567–6171.

There are lots of stories—some true, some not—on Kauai, and those tales are explored by a 2½-hour tour offered by the North Shore Cab Company. The tour is entertaining and informative. Ask for the History, Myth, and Legend Tour; call 808/826–6189.

A number of unusual tours are offered on Oahu. Try the Historic Downtown Walking Tour offered by the Mission Houses Museum (808/531–0481), the Chinatown Walking Tour (808/533–3181), and the famous Polynesian Cultural Center, a Mormon-operated, 40-acre park that has seven recreated Polynesian villages, nonstop entertainment and demonstrations, and an evening dinner show (808/293–3333).

Costs start at $65 per person.

Sea Kayaking Trips

Sea kayaks are fast, maneuverable vessels that will allow you to get to places that are inaccessible by any other means.

Two groups offer trips that range from one- to five-day journeys along Kauai's dramatic Na Pali coast. Island Adventure has half-day trips (808/245–9662) and Adventure Kayaking International has five-day itineraries (808/941–9172).

On Molokai, Island Adventures (808/988–5515 or 800/63–ISLES) offers three-day tours of the scenic and turbulent north shore, complete with guide, food, and equipment.

On Oahu, Twogood Kayaks Hawaii offers exciting exploratory tours of the coastline (808/235–2352).

Kayaks rent for about $25 a half-day, $40 a full day. Guided tours are extra.

Nihau Tours

Nihau, the once forbidden island whose inhabitants still live in the nineteenth century, is now open for limited tours. The island is fascinating: its 200 residents speak only Hawaiian, there is no electricity, telephones, or other modern gadgets. Nihau Helicopters tours the western coastline, with two landings: one at a sunken volcanic crater and the second at a cliff overlooking a beach. Going off on your own, though, is still forbidden. Call 808/338-1234. The cost starts at $135 per person.

Sailing Away

There is nothing more romantic or restful as a pleasant sail. And in the islands, Maui is the center of sailing. Call Scotch Mist Charters (808/661-0386), Seabern Yachts (808/661-8110), Genesis Sailing Charters (808/667-5667), and Sail Hawaii (808/879-2201).

From Maui you can also sail to Lanai's Club Lanai, a private beach on the island. The cruise includes breakfast on board, lunch, bus tours of island sights, and water sports. Call 808/871-1144.

On Oahu, try Mauna Kai, a 50-foot catamaran that sails from Waikiki Beach at noon and 2:00 PM and at 5:30 PM for a sunset cruise (808/923-1234, ext. 6300).

The Silver Cloud Limousine Service can arrange a private yacht charter. Call 808/524-7999. And Tradewind Charters offers three-hour sunset sails with champagne and other goodies. Call 808/533-0220.

From Molokai, Whistling Swan Charters conducts three-day sails along the north shore (808/553-5238).

On Hawaii, Captain Bean's offers daily sunset dinner cruises from the Kailua-Kona wharf (808/329-2955).

Art Tours

Maui is famed for the quality of the work of the artists who live on the island. You can tour the homes of some of these artists and talk with them over a spot of tea. The tour, conducted by limousine, includes a very charming lunch. The cost is $150 per person. Call 808/572–8374.

The My-Time-Is-Limited Tour

If your time is limited but you don't want to miss anything, contact Action Hawaii Adventures, which holds day-long tours that hit all the high spots, from rain forests to snorkeling to nature walks. Call 808/732–4453. The cost is $25 to $65 per person.

The sea is one of the routine hazards at Hawaii's golf courses.
(Photo courtesy of Patti Cook & Associates)

CHAPTER 8

Golf and Tennis

*H*awaii's magnificent golf courses have long attracted the world's top players, and the state is also beginning to build a reputation as a major tennis center with the development of the Wailea Tennis Center on Maui.

There are more than 60 golf courses on the islands, and more are expected to open in the 1990s. The courses are as beautiful as they are challenging, and only about a dozen of them are closed to the public.

The gorgeous courses and the inviting weather attract the pros and top amateurs. The GTE Kaanapali Classic Pro Am Golf Tournament hosts the PGA seniors in December on Maui, the Hawaiian Open is in January at the private Waialae Country Club in Honolulu, and the LPGA Women's Kemper Open is in Wailea on Maui in February.

The Wailea Tennis Club on Maui is nicknamed Wimbledon West, because it has 14 courts—three grass courts (the only ones in the state) and 11 Plexipave. The center has lighted courts and an amphitheater stadium for watching matches. The location on the lush, landscaped hillside above the Wailea resort and the ocean makes the center one of the more beautiful sports facilities in the islands.

The hotels and resorts give preference to their guests, but do admit nonguests when tee times and courts are available. Call first to check availability and costs. A rundown of the golf courses and tennis centers, listed by island, follows.

Hawaii

The Best Golf Courses on the Island:

The Kona Country Club—This course in Kailua-Kona was designed by William Bell and has 27 holes, with each nine-hole course having a par of 33. An 18-hole round can be as long as 6,800 yards if you take the two longest nines. Call 808/322-2595.

Mauna Kea Beach Resort—Designed by Robert Trent Jones, Sr., this 18-hole, par-72, 6,781-yard course is incredibly beautiful: black lava fields, magnificent fairways and greens, lush landscaping, and views of the real Mauna Kea make it a visual stunner. Call 808/882-7222.

Mauna Lani Bay Hotel—The Frances I'i Brown Golf Course at this west coast resort is among the finest in the state. The course has 18 holes, a par of 72, and is 6,259 yards. The greens and fairways undulate through the rough black lava fields surrounding the resort. The sixth hole is famous: the ball must carry over the ocean to reach the green. Call 808/885-6655.

Waikoloa Beach Golf Club—Robert Trent Jones, Jr., designed the links here out of the black lava fields, ancient fishing villages, and burial grounds adjacent to the Sheraton Royal Waikoloan. The course has 18 holes, a par of 71, and is 6,003 yards long. Call 808/885-6060.

Waikoloa Kings Course—This new 18-hole course at the Hyatt Regency Waikoloan has a par of 72 and is 6,594 yards long. It was designed by PGA star Tom Weiskopf and Associates. Call 808/885-6060.

Elsewhere on Hawaii:

Other courses include the Waikoloa Village Golf Course in South Kohala (created by Robert Trent Jones, Jr.), 808/883-9621; the nine-hole Hamakua Country Club in Honokaa, 808/775-7244; the Hilo Municipal Golf Course, 808/959-7711; Volcano Golf and Country Club in the national park, 808/967-7331; and Sea Mountain Golf Club, 808/928-6222.

The Best Tennis Courts on Hawaii:

Hoolulu Park—Eight courts, three lighted, at this tennis complex a mile from the Hilo waterfront. Call 808/961-9868.

King Kamehameha—Four Laykold courts, two lighted. Call 808/329-2911.

Mauna Kea Beach Resort—Thirteen Plexipave courts in a tennis complex listed among the top 50 complexes in the nation by *Tennis* magazine. Call 808/882-7222.

Mauna Lani Bay Hotel—The ten-court Tennis Garden was selected as Court of the Year by *Tennis Industry* magazine in 1988. Call 808/885-6622.

Sheraton Royal Waikoloan—Six courts with instructors. Call 808/885-6789.

Kauai

The Best Golf Courses on the Island:

Kiahuna Golf Club—Robert Trent Jones, Jr., designed this rather flat south shore course. It has 18 holes, with a par of 70 and 5,631 yards (6,353 yards from the championship tees). Two additional 18-hole courses and another 9-hole course are planned. Call 808/742-9595.

Princeville Makai Golf—This north shore complex in Hanalei has three nine-hole courses—called Lakes, Ocean, and Woods—created by Robert Trent Jones, Jr., and utilizes every obstacle from the ocean to jungle caverns to Zen gardens. The par-36 nines can be combined to make 18-hole rounds of par 72, with lengths from 6,164 to 6,284 yards. Call 808/826-3580.

Princeville Prince Course—You can combine a 9-hole round at this 18-hole, par-72, 5,433-yard course with any of the nines at the Makai course. Call 808/826-6561.

Westin Kauai—Jack Nicklaus is director of golf at the Westin and designed its two golf courses. The Kauai Lagoons course—18 holes, par 72, 6,392 yards—was ranked among the top ten new resort courses in 1989 by *Golf* magazine, while the Kiele course—18 holes, par 72, 7,070 yards—was called America's best new resort course in the same year. Call 808/245-5061.

Elsewhere, try the Wailua Municipal Golf Course in Lihue. Call 808/245-8092.

The Best Tennis Courts on Kauai:

Coco Palms Resort—Nine courts, two lighted. Call 808/822–3831.

Hanalei Bay Resort—Eleven Laykold resorts, three lighted, in a beautiful setting on the north shore. Call 808/826–6522.

Kiahuna Plantation—Ten courts, seven with lights, at this Poipu Beach complex. Call 808/742–9533.

Princeville Tennis Center—Six Plexipave courts, three lighted, at this north shore center. Call 808/826–6561.

Stouffer Waiohai Tennis Club—Six Laykold courts, four lighted, with instructors at this Poipu Beach center. Call 808/742–9511.

Lanai

The Best Golf Courses on the Island:

The Lodge at Koele—A new 18-hole course designed by Greg Norman and Ted Robinson opens in 1991. Call 808/548–3768.

The Manele Bay Hotel—If all permits come through, this new hotel, opening in late 1991, will also have an 18-hole Jack Nicklaus course. Call 808/548–3768.

The best tennis courts are also at the Lodge at Koele and the Manele Bay Hotel.

Maui

The Best Golf Courses on the Island:

Kapalua Golf Club—The two 18-hole courses at this west shore resort were designed by Arnold Palmer. A third course, opening around 1991, was designed by Ben Crenshaw. The connection to the PGA becomes clear every November when the Isuzu Kapalua International Tournament is held at the club. The

Bay Course is 18 holes, par 72, 6,180 yards. The Village Course is 18 holes, par 71, 6,194 yards. Call 808/669–8044.

Makena Golf Course—Robert Trent Jones, Jr., designed this 18-hole, par-72, 6,210-yard course in Kihei. The narrow fairways, fast greens, 64 bunkers, and four ponds make it a real test. Call 808/879–3344.

Royal Kaanapali Golf Courses—Robert Trent Jones, Sr., designed the north course—18 holes, par 72, 6,305 yards—and Arthur Jack Snyder designed the south course—18 holes, par 72, 6,250 yards—at this popular west coast resort. Call 808/661–3691.

Wailea Golf Club—Arthur Jack Snyder designed both the Blue and Orange courses at this popular club, where the fairways are narrow and the greens are elevated. The Blue is 18 holes, par 72, 6,327 yards, and the Orange is 18 holes, par 72, 6,405 yards. Call 808/879–2966.

The Best Tennis Courts on Maui:

The Wailea Tennis Club—The finest in the state and the world, this 14-court complex is often called Wimbledon West. There are 3 grass courts and 11 Plexipave courts. Three courts have lights. Pros available. Call 808/879–1958.

The Royal Lahaina Tennis Ranch—Eleven courts, six lighted, with pro instructors. Call 808/661–3611.

Elsewhere on the island, the Hyatt Regency Maui has five courts, 808/661–1234; the Kapalua Tennis Gardens has ten courts, four lighted, 808/669–5677; and the Maui Marriott has five courts, three lighted, 808/667–1200.

Molokai

The Best Golf Course on the Island:

Kaluakoi Golf Course—Ted Robinson designed the 18-hole, par-72, 6,618-yard course at this resort. Call 808/552–2739.

The best tennis courts (four, all lighted) are also at the Kaluakoi Hotel & Golf Club on the western end of the island. Call 808/552–2739.

Oahu

The Best Golf Courses on the Island:

Makaha Valley—The two courses at this western shore resort are near the Sheraton Makaha Resort. The courses, designed by William Bell, are the hotel's own West Course—par 72, 18 holes, 6,400 yards (808/695-9511)—and the Makaha Valley Country Club—par 72, 18 holes, 6,530 yards (808/695-9578). The courses are superbly maintained and while the fairways are fair, the greens can be killers.

Turtle Bay Hilton and Country Club—George Fazio designed the par-72, 6,366-yard, 18-hole course at this windward coast resort, and his talents have managed to hide its deficit—a flat location—with skillful use of trees, traps and water. A second 18-hole course is planned. Call 808/293-8811.

Elsewhere, try these popular public courses: The Ali Wai Golf Course at the north end of Waikiki, 808/296-4653; Hawaii Kai Golf Course and the nine-hole Hawaii Kai Executive Course in Honolulu, 808/395-2358; and the Olomana Golf Links in Waimanalo, 808/259-7926.

The Best Tennis Courts on Oahu:

Hawaiian Regent Hotel—One court at this Waikiki hotel, with lessons from the acclaimed Peter Burwash. International pros. Call 808/922-6611.

Honolulu Tennis Club—Four Laykold courts on a third-floor rooftop location. One pro. Pickup service from many Waikiki hotels. Call 808/944-9696.

Ilikai—Seven Plexipave courts, including one lighted, on the ballroom roof of the Ilikai Waikiki Hotel. Two staff pros. Call 808/949-3811.

Pacific Beach Hotel—Two courts with instructors at this Waikiki resort. Call 808/922-1233.

Sheraton Makaha—Four Plexipave courts, two lighted. Few crowds because of its western shore location. Call 808/695-9511.

Turtle Bay Hilton—Ten Plexipave courts, including four lighted for night play. Call 808/293–8811.

Golf and Tennis Tournaments

Hawaiian Open Golf Tournament—Waialae Country Club Golf Course. January.

Orix Hawaiian Ladies Open—Ko Olina Golf Course, Oahu. February.

Asahi Beer Kyosan Golf Tournament—Men and women pros compete in this tournament at the Wailea Golf Course on Maui. February.

LPGA Women's Kemper Open Golf Tournament—Women pros compete at Wailea on Maui. February.

Kapalua Tennis Junior Vet/Senior Championship—Men and women over 35 compete at the Tennis Garden on Maui. May.

Kona Golf Classic—18-hole men's and women's tournament featuring two-player teams and four-ball format at the Kona Country Club on Hawaii. June.

Hawaii State Clay Court Championships—Part of the Kauai Grand Prix circuit at the Coco Palms Resort. June.

Mauna Kea Beach Hotel's Pro-Am Golf Tournament—A 54-hole event with 30 teams. July.

Wailea Open Tennis Tournament—A stop on the Hawaii Grand Prix circuit, at the Wailea Tennis Club on Maui. July.

Kapalua Open Tennis Tournament—Another Hawaii Grand Prix event, at the Tennis Garden on Kauai. September.

Hawaii Grand Prix Championships—The final stop on the Grand Prix tour, at the Turtle Bay Hilton. October.

Nissan Hawaii Open—At the Ala Moana Tennis Center in Honolulu. October.

Waikoloa Open Golf Tournament—Top pros and amateurs from the islands compete at the Waikoloa courses on Hawaii. October.

Isuzu Kapalua International Championship Golf—Top pros compete at the Kapalua Resort on Maui. November.

Kapalua Betsy Nagelson Pro-Am Tennis Invitational—Top field of women players compete at the Kapalua Resort on Maui. November.

Ted Malakena State Open—Top island golfers compete at the Ala Wai Golf Course in Waikiki. November.

Mauna Kea Beach Hotel's Invitational Golf Tournament—54-hole medal play for men, 36-hole event for women. December.

GTE Kaanapali Classic Pro Am Golf Tournament—Grand finale of the seniors tour at the Kaanapali Beach Resort. December.

For more information and specific dates, call the Hawaii Visitors' Bureau at 808/923–1811.

CHAPTER 9

Ways and Means

*I*f you have never visited Hawaii before, you will be confronted with different climates, diverse lifestyles, and some transportation obstacles. So before you visit Hawaii, there are a number of things you may want to consider, beyond the obvious: Which island? These issues include when to go, how to cut costs, the best way to get around an island and to travel between islands, and what to take with you.

When to Go

Hawaii's high season is from mid-December through mid-April, the time when winter-weary mainlanders fly to the islands for sun and fun.

Winter in the islands is very pleasant, with a few more showers than in other seasons. Keep in mind that there's usually more rain on the northern and eastern shores of the islands, and that Kauai and the Big Island get more rain than the other islands.

Even in the winter months, temperatures remain fairly balmy, with average daytime highs around 80 degrees and lows in the low 60s on all islands. That's only about 4 to 7 degrees less than the average highs and lows recorded during the summer season. The summer highs can hit the low 90s, but the tradewinds usually make this bearable. When the winds are not present, though, the heat can be stifling.

There is another difference in the winter and summer seasons. The big waves of the north Pacific roll into Oahu's north shore during winter, turning the placid bays of summer into a competition field of 30-foot-high waves that attracts surfers from all over the world.

The final big difference between winter and summer on the islands is the number of visitors. Winter is the busy season, the time when the most popular resorts are booked solid for months ahead of time. During the summer months, these same resorts often have rooms available at the last minute. The differences in rates between the seasons isn't much, with summer rates averaging only about 10 to 15 percent less than the winter rates. That's a much smaller drop-off in seasonal rates than that found in Florida or the Caribbean. The airline fares are also more expensive in the winter than in the summer.

All these factors—weather, seasonal rates, availability of rooms and airline seats—add up to choosing wisely when planning your trip. It may be more fun to get away to Hawaii during the cold of winter, but it will also be more expensive and will require longer-range planning.

Cutting Costs

The ultimate romantic journey would not take cost into consideration. But almost all of us live in the real world, the one of budgets, and you can still have a very romantic visit to Hawaii just by following a few suggestions. First, we attempted to list inexpensive and moderate resorts and restaurants when possible on the islands. Second, the room rates quoted in this book are based on how much you would pay if you booked a room for one night at those resorts. The rates serve only as a guide to the cost of the resort, not a hard-and-fast indicator of how much you would pay if you stayed longer, booked your visit as part of a tour, or used a number of other methods to cut costs.

These cost-cutters include:

• If you want to go to a particular resort, ask about their special packages. Most of the larger resorts offer cost-cutting deals labeled golf. tennis, or honeymoon packages. These rates usually include a meal plan, all the golf or tennis you want, and other goodies. The savings can be as much as half of what you would pay if you just called the resort and booked a room.

• Check with your travel agent, the tour desks of major airlines like United and American, and the travel magazines and travel sections of major newspapers for package tours that include air, four- to seven-day stays at usually a well-known resort, a car, and meals. The savings can be considerable.

American Fly AAway Vacations (800/443–7300), Delta Airlines (800/221–6666), and United Vacations (800/328–6877) can tell you more about their packages. American Express Vacations (800/241–1700), Maupintour (800/255–4266), Pleasant Hawaiian Holidays (800/2-HAWAII), and Trieloff Tours (800/432–7125) are major tour operators that offer their own package plans. Before you call them, have a firm idea of which island(s) you wish to visit. The more money you wish to save, the more flexible you must be in choosing which resort you will visit.

• When renting a car on the islands, ask the rental agency if they have any discount deals at hotels. Often they do, and this car/room package can save enough to pay for the car rental. The car agencies also give away driving guides that have discount coupons to numerous attractions, restaurants, and tours.

• Discount travel clubs can save you up to 50 percent on the cost of a tour package. These clubs, most of which charge small annual membership fees, buy up unsold tour packages from travel wholesalers and they offer them to their members at steep discounts. The catch is that the trips are often—but not always—offered on as short as a few days' notice. This may not be for you, but if you are able to get away on short notice, the savings they offer may be worth investigating.

Some of the larger clubs and their fees are Discount Travel International (215/668–2182, annual fee $45); Encore Short Notice (301/459–8020, $48); Last-Minute Travel Club (800/LAST-MIN, $30 per person, $35 per family); Moments Notice (212/486–0503, $45); Stand Buys Ltd. (800/255–1487, $45 per family), and Worldwide Discount Travel Club (305/534–2082, $40 a person, $50 per family).

Getting Around

Most visitors fly to the islands, and most arrive at Honolulu International Airport. From there you can take Aloha Airlines (800/

367–5250) or Hawaiian Airlines (800/367–5320) to every island but Lanai (although that might change when Lanai's airport is expanded). Aloha Island Air (800/323–3345) flies from Honolulu to Lanai and all the other islands. Both of these carriers offer dependable, regular air service between the islands.

Once in the islands, a car is a must on Hawaii, Maui, Molokai, Kauai, and Oahu, if you want to explore outside the cities and resort areas. Lanai is small, the roads are often rugged dirt trails, and the routes are not well marked. On this island we suggest taking a four-wheel-drive guided tour. Book one through your hotel.

Finding the landscape you desire may be easier if you remember that the islands have a wet side where the vegetation is lush and a dry side where the vegetation is nice, but less verdant. The northern and eastern shores of the islands are the wet coasts, while the southern and western shores are the dry sides.

Most of the roads on the islands are well paved and maintained, as long as you are going between population and resort centers. If your idea of fun is exploring the rain forests, driving to the summits of volcanoes, wandering off on dirt and rock roads, you will need a four-wheel-drive vehicle.

The islands have all the major car rental firms: Avis (800/331–1212), Budget (800/527–0707), Dollar (800/367–7006), Hertz (800/654–8200), National (800/CAR-RENT), and Thrifty (800/367–2277). Most rent cars, vans, and jeeps, and Budget also rents golf clubs.

At all times, check your auto insurance policy to see if it covers you when you drive a rental car. Some gold cards (Visa and American Express) also automatically cover you for the collision damage if you charge the car on their card. In short, don't sign up for the damage waiver unless you are certain you are not covered by your existing policy or credit card agreement. Don't expect the car rental agency to help you save yourself $10–$14 a day.

What to Pack

This depends on what type of resort you are visiting and the time of year you visit. The few very elegant hotels and resorts have a main dining room with a dress code for dinner. The code usually requires jackets and shirts with collars (and sometimes even a tie) for men and dresses or pant suits for women. If this seems too much trouble during the humid summer months, consider eating at the less chic dining rooms at the resort. Most dining rooms request "casual elegance" with the emphasis on casual. Some restaurants have an aloha attire, which means very casual attire, up to flowered shirts and shorts.

Otherwise, pack according to the activities you plan to enjoy on the islands. If you want to visit the volcano summits on Maui or Hawaii, take along sweaters and jackets. The temperatures on top of the mountains can be in the 30s and 40s even during the summer. Take a sweater or wrap for the evening in the winter.

If you like to hike in the rough forests, bring appropriate shoes and old clothes. The rain forests are aptly named, for the environment is wet, humid, and muddy, and the going can be difficult without the proper gear.

At all times, bring along heavy-duty sunscreen, sunglasses, cameras and film (the sunsets are outstanding), and swimsuits.

What to Take Home

Shopping is often a major component of our getaways. Even though we don't buy much, just looking at the different crafts, works of art, local produce, and other items is fun.

Hawaii is famous for its wood bowls, trays, and other items made from the koa, mango, and monkeypod trees. Other popular items include macadamia nuts (regular, chocolate-covered, and in candy and cookies); Kona coffee; shell leis, and jewelry ranging from inexpensive coral rings and necklaces to lavish creations of gold, pearls, diamonds, and other precious stones that can cost a king's ransom. Maui is the home of many artists who sell their creations in the island shops. The gaily colored Aloha shirts, muumuus, and T-shirts are found almost everywhere.

A Question of Time

The islands are on Hawaiian Standard Time, which means that the islands are two hours earlier than California and five hours earlier than the East Coast; Hawaii does not observe daylight savings time, so from late April through late October the islands are three hours earlier than California and six hours earlier than New York City.

Businesses generally open early in the islands, with most offices and small business opening from 8:00 AM to 5:00 PM. Banks usually are open from 8:30 AM to 3:00 PM or 3:30 PM (with some branches staying open until 6:00 PM on Fridays), and shopping malls are open from 9:30 AM or 10:00 AM until 9:00 PM.

Index

General Index

Hotels